T0354396

8000 Feet Over Hell

Peter Constandelis

Order this book online at www.trafford.com
or email orders@trafford.com

Most Trafford titles are also available at major online book retailers.

Print information available on the last page.

ISBN: 978-1-4251-3346-7 (sc)
ISBN: 978-1-4251-3348-1 (hc)

Trafford rev. 08/08/2018

www.trafford.com
North America & international
toll-free: 1 888 232 4444 (USA & Canada)
fax: 812 355 4082

Acknowledgments

First, I would like to thank my wife of 60 years, Theodora, for her patience, understanding, and tolerance. Without her assistance, this book would have never materialized. She was not thrilled with my writing this book at the kitchen table, and more than once I got myself into hot water for the clutter I left in my makeshift office.

I would also like to thank my son Peter, whose assistance in jogging my memory, outlining, rearranging, and countless hours delving deeper into the subject matter helped orchestrate this book.. I would also like to thank Mrs. Phyllis Gigantes, Councilwoman, from Wayne, New Jersey, for her assistance, and also the Jewish War Veterans of Wayne for selecting me as their Air Force Grand Marshal during the Memorial Day Parade, 2004.

I would also like to give thanks to my daughter-in-law, Patricia E. Palermo, PhD., for assistance with grammar, and to the late Mr. Don Sweet for his input .

Finally, above all, I dedicate this book to my comrades of the 20th Air Force, many of whom made the ultimate sacrifice.

My thanks to you all.

Nick Constandelis

TABLE OF CONTENTS

_____

Chapter I

Leaving Home, and Being Inducted into the U.S. Army

I remember that beautiful sunny March morning in 1943 as if it were yesterday. The long winter was over, and there was crispness in the spring morning air. The sun shone brightly and there was a fresh scent of nature that filled the air. I awoke bright and early, almost too early, as I had gotten to bed late lastnight, and was unable to fall asleep. I lay there tossing and turning for a while, unable to get comfortable, my mind racing with thoughts of what life might have instore for me. I'm sure it wasn't till the wee hours of morning that I finally drifted off to sleep and all too soon, the rays of sunlight in my bedroom woke me.

I opened the window as wide as possible, and took a deep breath. It felt so good to fill my lungs with fresh air, and it helped get rid of the cobwebs in my head from the lack of sleep. I thought of those horrible snowy days of winter that had so complicated my commute to work in New York City, and now with spring here they were finally over. The thoughts of getting up in darkness, being so cold while waiting for the train, or trudging through snow to get either home or to the station were over for at least another year. As I gazed out the window I thought about how wonderful the change from winter to spring is. Aside from the fact that we all suffer from a sort of Cabin Fever as we wait for the transition to spring, its arrival is like an elixir that comes just in the nick of time. It sort of gives you a new perspective on life, as the trees come alive again and the whole cycle of life begins anew

It seems that my life was also facing a period of extreme change. At 22 years of age, I was about to say goodbye to my family and felt real concern in doing so. I was quick to rise, shower and shave, and have breakfast with all of them, and begin the emotional goodbyes. After the hugs and kisses from my family, and feeling a bit choked-up, I hastened my departure and began my walk downtown.

As I walked, preoccupied with thoughts of what was to come, I passed first the high school, then the elementary school that I had attended in my youth, but I wasn't thinking much of school days. Instead, my thoughts were on my family, and that they had all come over last night to wish me well, and that it was so nice having seen everyone. I had gotten to bed late, by the time all the company had left, and my bout with insomnia left me somewhat sleep deprived.

I continued on my way with a host of thoughts flying through my mind, and was jostled into reality rather abruptly by my sister Connie and our cousin Ann as they ran to catch up with me. As a matter of fact, I was so deep in thought that they startled me as they joined me. Hearing their footsteps close behind, I turned quickly, and jumped from the surprise of them being there. They laughed at my reaction, and as I calmed down a bit they said they had been calling me for some time, but I hadn't heard them. Obviously my thoughts were elsewhere, and they sensed my edginess, and tried hard to uplift my spirits. We walked together, laughing and talking the whole way, which made the trip to the YMCA on Ward Street a pleasant one. That trip downtown was made in record time, at least that's how it felt to me.

I was to meet a military bus at that location, and the girls cheerfully waited with me, standing with the families of other recruits. Within 10 minutes the bus pulled up, and a Sergeant emerged, reading names from his roster sheet. We were instructed to board the bus as our names were called. Upon hearing my name, I said my goodbyes to the girls, and boarded the bus.

Without looking back, I heard,

"You better not forget to write, we'll be waiting to hear from you" my sister Connie shouted, as I nodded in acknowledgment and waved goodbye.

Weeks earlier I had received my draft notice through the mail, and was instructed to report to the local service board in Paterson, New Jersey. I recall coming home from work and seeing the letter from the local draft board, and knowing full well what it was about. I wasn't surprised, but I felt somewhat anxious while reading it. I had to translate it for my parents explaining that I had been drafted and most likely would soon be in the service. They were not happy at all about the news, although since the attack of Pearl Harbor I had entertained the notion of enlisting.

Whenever the topic arose I was always dissuaded by my parents, and told of my obligations and that I was an essential part of the family, and that I was needed here. I'm sure it wasn't my parents lack of patriotism that impacted this decision, but more the economics of the times, and their concern for my safety.

Upon reporting, I was issued my papers and told to report for active duty in 2 weeks; that was in March of 1943. From that day that's all that was on my mind. This would change my life in ways that I could never imagine.

Having been born in 1921 and having faced the economic hardships of the Great Depression, we all did our part in helping and contributing to the family. There were no options, that's just the way things were, and my childhood ended rather abruptly. Being the oldest in my family, I began working at selling newspapers on the street corner until 1:A.M. to help contribute to the family. I turned over all the money I collected to my parents, and continued to do so for many years. This work ethic began when I was 10 years old, and continued at a seven-day-a-week pace until my indoctrination into the service.

I was forced to grow up quickly, and became street wise to survive. But this fast decent into maturity also had its downside. I would be the first in my family to serve my country, and felt very proud in doing so, but was somewhat naive about it. I knew nothing about what to expect, only what I had read in the newspapers and the stories that I had heard of basic training were

2

mostly told in joking manners solely for entertainment. Needless to say, it was somewhat troubling, but I guess I would learn from first hand experience. I notified my employer of my draft status and that I would be leaving to serve my time in the service.

We soon arrived in Newark and stopped at one other location to pick up the remainder of the recruits, and then went on to Newark's Penn Station. Upon our arrival, the Sergeant ran inside and we were instructed to wait on the bus. He returned within minutes with train tickets that he passed out to us, and we were instructed to meet at Penn's main entrance area in twenty minutes. We were all dressed in civilian clothing and as I looked around, I couldn't help but notice that some fellows had brought suitcases with them. I couldn't see the logic in their carrying luggage on this trip, after all, this was no vacation. Anyway I passed time making small talk and looking through the crowd to see if I knew anyone there. It would be nice to see a familiar face, but unfortunately, there was no one there of my acquaintance.

Train travel was the most convenient form of transportation at that time, especially if traveling any distance, and I'm sure the government had worked out a deal with the rail road for our transport. However, this train was not designated exclusively for the armed services, and we shared the trip with the regular commuters. There were civilians, the every day commuters, and regular working people that normally used the train and then add us to that equation, and it equals a crowd. We boarded at the specified time, squeezed into whatever space was available and began the trip and my new life, one that would start at Fort Dix, N.J. with my orientation.

The train emptied to a comfortable capacity after the first few stops, and soon the only passengers left on board were recruits. I relaxed and took in the beautiful sights of southern New Jersey. There were vast pine forests, farms and much wildlife in this beautiful undeveloped area. I was amazed at the vastness of the landscape. That trip was long, and to pass the time during the ride, I looked out the window and thought about what was to come. That first hour was kind of strange in the respect of the range of thoughts and emotions that go through your mind.

I was on my own: there was a war going on that I had been drafted into. With that came the probability that I would inevitably face potentially fatal situations in the near future. That was something that I had never thought of, and it kind of jolted me a little. At 22 years of age, I was tough, almost invincible, and could take on or do almost anything. I guess all men of this age group sort of mask the truth about fear, especially fear of this nature. There's something about the male ego and mind set in that age group, whether it's stupidity, or the competitive nature of men that makes them perfect candidates for the military. However, the facade we portray isn't always the way things really are for us. I was a little worried about the prospects of dodging lead but tried not to think about it or show it.

Upon arriving at Fort Dix, in typical military manner, we were told to hurry up and wait. That is one of the truisms of life, especially in the military, and that never changes. We were shuffled inside and out, moved here and there and of course were made to wait for what seemed to be hours. During this process we were told to wait outside for a while, and after a while it began to get cold, very cold. The sun began to set and as the temperature plummeted most of us looked for some source of warmth. I might have been drafted, but I was no fool. I went inside and waited with a few others, while most other recruits just sat there shivering in the cold night air. The Army did finally get around to outfitting us with a complete basic Army uniform including hats, socks, and shoes; everything we would need. The pants were too long and the shoes a half size too big, anyone who has been in the service at that time knows what I'm talking about We were given a box for all our civilian clothing to be shipped home. It was made quite clear to us that we wouldn't need these clothes again, not for a very long time. We were oriented, given three shots, showed our quarters for sleeping and told where to report for food. We ate some dinner and got to bed early and were awakened in the early hours of the A.M.

Those first few days took some getting used to. While not difficult, the military routine was implemented as we were now the property of the U.S. Army. Physicals and countless immunizations and medical history questionnaires were filled out. After all the data was compiled, we were interviewed and asked what our occupations had been before we were drafted. During my interview, I spoke of my employment by MW Kellogg Co, where I was employed as a Design Draftsman. I explained in detail my duties and designs within the industry, but this guy was writing as I spoke, not paying much attention to what I was saying, so I paused, and waited for him to look up at me.

It dawned on me that this guy wasn't interested in what I did; he was looking for the best place for me to serve. Understanding that the interview was for placement purposes, my mind raced with thoughts of what branch of the service I should be placed in.

I thought that I wouldn't be a very good foot soldier, carrying that thirty pound backpack, and me being so thin, not for me. It is strange how your mind works, as these thoughts rocket through your head, and you speak without missing a beat of the conversation.

Air Force, flying in airplanes: that might be for me, I thought. I would enjoy having something to do with flight.

"All right now, what about hobbies, do you have any?" asked the Sergeant.

"As a matter of fact, I love airplanes, and since I was a kid I was fascinated with flight and read everything I could get my hands on about airplanes."

I had seen a few airplanes as a young kid in a nearby airport, on a church picnic, and they had influenced me tremendously. I remember my father took me for a walk after the picnic through the fields until we were close to the runway, and we saw an old airplane up close. I looked inside this beautiful machine, and felt the urge to climb aboard and into the pilot's seat, just to see what it was like.

"Can I go inside it?" I asked my father about entering the plane. He smiled and shook his head no. But he did lift me up so I could sit on the wing.

From that point on I was hooked, even the thought of flying, invoked this feeling of euphoria and freedom, especially to a youngster of the Depression generation. "I often thought about what it would be like behind the controls, in the cockpit of one of those machines, and even did a book report in school about airplanes."

I guess my passion, and enthusiasm about planes and flight was enough to influence the Sergeant, because as I looked up at him, he had a smile on his face. His hand covered half the smile partially, but he nodded, put down his pen and concluded the interview.

Following that interview, I was assigned to the Army Air Corps.

I felt great about my placement, and even being in the Army, and was comfortable in knowing that I wouldn't be walking as an infantryman in the trenches carrying a backpack.

We spent a total of 28 days at Fort Dix, where the majority of time was used as an assessment period; determining placement for the greatest potential of service would be realized. We did some physical training throughout our stay, including a long indoctrination into the finer aspects of K.P. This included washing large pots and pans, and peeling hundreds of potatoes, including every other aspect of Army life imaginable.

We were lectured on all facets of the military, and were told what was expected of us, as we began the transformation into soldiers.

We also had some down time where we managed to hone our card skills at the art of poker during the stay. Some of these guys were very good at playing cards, and I soon realized that a few of them were always winning the pots. These chosen few seemed to have developed a knack of knowing when to fold on a hand, and I had my suspicion that there might have been some collaboration between a few of them. Not that these were colossal kitty's, the majority of the games were a nickel a hand or so but I still got a bad feeling about a few of these guys.

"All right now, let's separate the men from the boys…..I raise a quarter" said Jones.

"I'll see that raise, but lets make it a little more interesting, it's a half to you now, Jonesie," replied Garth.

"Too rich for my blood," as the other two players folded.

"All right, Jonesie, looks like it's just the two of us, I call."

"Well looks like I got a pair of deuces staring me in the face," as Jones laid down the pair…. "Oh did I say a pair …sorry, I meant to say two pair" as Jones lays down a second pair with a slight grin on his face.

"Wow" Garth replied, looking somewhat bewildered, "Gee two pair, pretty good hand Jonesie"…….as Garth seemed to relinquish the Kitty.

Jones face begins to light up, as the grin broadens into an ear to ear smile. Almost gloating he reaches for the pot, and just as his hand touches it, Garth continues.

"But three smiling ladies beat two pair as I recall" as he lays down three queens in the most artful manner.

"I want to thank you gentlemen for your contribution to the foundation, the Garth retirement foundation that is," he commented smugly as he pulled the booty toward his pile.

That was enough for the evening for most of us, as we retired for the evening, some cursing, some in awe of what had just happened. Anyway, tomorrow was another day.

After three and a half weeks of being there, I learned who to avoid getting into card games with, although, like anything else, you learn from experience, and those lessons are expensive. It was around this time we learned that we would soon be issued our orders for our basic training, and the location would be determined by which branch of the service we were placed in.

These were some exotic places, or so I thought, and I was very much looking forward to traveling to a new destination. So as luck would have it, I was called to report with a group of men that were to be placed in the Army Air Force, and was instructed to board a train the next morning for Miami Beach, Florida.

With my new orders in hand, the following morning I boarded a train for Miami to undergo basic training. That was a Monday, March 29th, 1943. Was I ever excited, I had only read of Miami and now I would get a chance to experience first hand what it was like. Having been raised during the great depression, the furthest distance I had ever traveled was to New York City, and that was for work. I can't begin to tell you how elated I felt to be going there. I had met new friends and we were all happy about going to Miami Beach.

The trip was long and exhausting, as we rode in day coaches for the 36 hour trip. These were out and out uncomfortable, as our seats would also have to serve as beds and conditions were cramped. I shared my seat with, Bob Cooke, another GI from New Jersey who had the uncanny ability to fall asleep anywhere, and at any time. You could be in a conversation with this guy, and by the time you answered him, he would be snoring. How this guy got into the Air Force was a mystery, and I thought to myself, I hope this guys not going to be a pilot.

I don't know if he suffered from some sort of ailment, a predisposition to narcolepsy or was just tired all the time, but when this guy snored, he could peel the paint off the walls.

I did manage to get a total of 8 hours sleep within the two nights of travel, and everyone around us shared in the discomfort. Many became somewhat bothered by the lack of sleep, while others just made the best of it.

Those that were irritated about it started a campaign to end the noise by first nudging, and prodding Sleeping Beauty in an effort to get him to stop the snoring. These efforts were usually successful for a minute or two, and then it was back to the same racket.

"I'm going to shove a dirty sock in old Cook's mouth if he doesn't't stop soon" said one of the group.

"That won't work, I've already tried it, and he almost swallowed the sock. Lets give him a hot foot instead, that'll stop him" said another.

That didn't't seem right to do that to anyone, but we all had a good laugh about it and continued on with the trip. Most of the time the windows were all wide open, and on more than one occasion we were inundated with smoke and the stench of soot from the engine as it entered into the passengers compartments. We kept ourselves occupied by playing the nickel a hand Poker game, or passed the time watching the countryside as we traveled through the poverty laden south. While this train was equipped with minimal comfort facilities, there was not enough room in the restrooms to shave, or even wash up a bit, so by the time we got to Miami, we were to say the least, a little ripe.

Chapter II

_____

Basic Training: Miami Beach

It was on April 1st 1943, at about 7:00 AM when we pulled into the station, and it was warm and humid adding to our discomfort. Some April Fools Day, we all joked around a bit. We were instructed to board waiting transport trucks, and were taken to the resort town of Miami Beach. We pulled up in front of the hotel which we were to be stationed at, and began to exit the truck with all our belongings. Hot, sweaty and dirty, all we wanted to do was get situated and cleaned up. As we approached the door of the hotel, weighted down with all our belongings, we were intercepted by a Sergeant and instructed to board yet another waiting vehicle. We were packed in that transport truck, so tightly, sweating profusely until a wave of nausea came over me as we were shuffled off to the 40th street supply depot to be issued our bedding supplies.

This building looked truly dilapidated, and from the design seemed to have been a hotel at one time. Its two large brass entry doors, discolored from lack of use, and the peeling paint contributed to the rundown appearance of the building. It was obvious that this place had seen its heyday years before and was most likely slated for the wrecking ball before being taken over by the government. With the front doors propped open, we entered the sweltering building, and moved to the end of a line that seemed not to move.

"What the hell are we doing now" I said to the GI standing next to me. He just looked and shook his head in disgust.

"Well at least old Cooke isn't here" he said as we all started laughing.

"I think he's still on the train", someone chimed in from behind.

Every window was wide open and it was still stifling inside. In an effort to ease the discomfort and the inadequate ventilation, large portable fans were working trying to create some sort of cross breeze. While these efforts had merit, they were unfortunately futile, and all the fans accomplished was to push hot stale air around.

Having come from the north east, I thought we would welcome this type of weather, but in truth I think the combination of lack of sleep, in conjunction with our inability to shower or shave made matters seem unbearable. As the line progressed at a snails pace, I saw through the lobby that the majority of the bedding was being distributed in the next room, so hopefully we would be out soon. The air was laden with the heavy stench of perspiration as we neared the distribution point, and I felt myself slipping away into almost a dreamlike state, when I heard someone call out my name both clearly and distinctively.

"Hey Nick, Nick Constandelis"

Being of Greek decent, my last name was always a tad problematic to most people; however, this person barked it out as if he were Zorba the Greek. As I turned in the direction of the voice, I focused on a familiar face, that of Eugene Miller, a neighbor of mine from Paterson, NJ.

With a big smile on his face Eugene shook my hand and said;

"You know I told your mother I'd look after you, but you didn't have to look for me your first day here," as he slapped me on the back

"Gene, what the hell are you doing here, I thought you were somewhere in Europe fighting the war, and with all the time you've spent in the military, I thought you'd be a general by now" I said to him.

The Millers lived directly across the street from us in Paterson and even though Eugene was slightly older than I was, we were still friends. I knew he had enlisted 2 years ago, but had no idea he was in the Quartermasters Corps.

"Well you know, the upper brass hasn't yet acknowledged my leadership abilities, but we're working on that" he said, although he was sporting two stripes.

"You know you look great. I guess it's this Miami weather, and that sun tan you've got, you know I think there going to put you in the movies after the war," I said to him.

"Hey you guys done with the love affair, can we just get our stuff and get out of here" came a voice from the next guy in line.

I took Genes address, and told him we should get together. We shook hands again after issuing me my bedding and we said our farewell.

"I'll tell your family I saw you, and that you were well. I've got a leave coming up and Ill be going home" he said.

"That'll be great" I replied.

It was embarrassing to have him see me so shabbily groomed, but the entire group of us looked this way, and from the looks of everyone else on these lines, I guess that it was the norm.

What were the odds that I'd run into him? Seeing someone from home was great, even though it was just briefly, at least my thoughts switched momentarily from the oppressive heat to family and friends.

I continued on my way as I neared the back of the tent, saw the exit and made a beeline towards the opening. What a relief as I hit the outside, I gasped the fresh air, and even though it was heavy with humidity, it was such a relief from the closeness of the inside. At this point we re-grouped, were herded back into the transport trucks and driven to what would be our home for the next few months.

I was assigned to the Marine Terrace on the corner of 27th and Collins Avenue. This was Miami's main street in those days, and was situated right next to the more famous, Billows Hotel. While small by today's standards, at only two stories tall, never the less it was very nice. I shared a beach front room on the ground floor with a couple of guys from Philadelphia,

Frankie and Joey.

After brief introductions, and some comment about the bedding depot, and where we were all from, I casually managed to stroll by the bathroom first.

Looking in, I saw modern bath, a stall shower about 10 towels, and I thought this is heaven.

Dropping all my supplies next to a bed, I made a beeline towards the shower and jumped in. I cranked the water up as fast as it could come out and immersed myself in the cooling liquid. It was such a great feeling to finally feel clean again, and I savored every second of the cool water rejuvenating me.

What a great place this hotel is, beach front accommodations, our own bathroom, and I was worried about being drafted I thought to myself.

"Hey, hurry up in there" came voices from the room with a pounding on the bathroom door, as my impatient room mates made an effort to speed up my progress. "And don't use up all of the hot water, I know about you Jersey guys."

"Yea, yea, give me a couple of minutes, I have heard about you guys from Philly too, but mostly the fact that you don't take showers, what is it, are you guys afraid of the water" I said as they continued the rapping on the door laughing. I guess that first day cemented our friendship.

Marine Terrace

Frankie and Joey were a couple of good guys born and raised in south side Philadelphia, and were about the same age as I was.

From what I gather, it was sort of the rough side of town, and these guys seemed a little rough and tumble, but needless to say they were both characters, and we all got along well. We all shared mutual interests, I guess all young men of this age have similar interests in common,….. women, ……….alcohol, …….and gambling, not necessarily in that order.

As we all settled into our room, getting things organized, we were miraculously rejuvenated from the sleep depravation, and intense heat we had been subjected to. The first thing we did

9

was to locate the mess hall had some chow, after all that was the first priority. Then following protocol, we completed all tasks, meetings and other duties that were required of us, and finally as we were getting antsy, had a look at the sights of Miami.

As I found out, the weather was normally not that oppressive, and we had just been lucky enough to arrive during one of those dog days that occasionally happen. We walked up and down the main street that first night and took in some of the sights, familiarized ourselves with this paradise on earth, and of course took a swim in the ocean.

The mess hall was located a short distance from our hotel, and was set up in cafeteria style to accommodate the vast numbers of servicemen, and at meal time we would assemble in front of the hotel and would all fall into place and march together to the mess hall.

Our routine was that of typical military fashion, we woke to reveille at 4:45 AM and had until 5:30 to shower, shave, and clean our rooms. Breakfast was from 5:30 till 6:15, and upon completion we would return to our rooms, re-check everything for inspection and by 6:45 would fall in and march to the drill field. We sang cadence on this march, kind of loudly, waking up all the civilians at this early hour. It gave us some pleasure sharing our early morning rising and activities with the general public; however the few vacationers that were trying to sleep-in did not share our enthusiasm in the early morning hours.

The A#$%*&%$?!#$%^&*! Comments coming from the open windows as we made our way to the drill field were anything but appreciative, but we found some humor in their off-color comments. Frankie especially got great pleasure in awakening the sleeping vacationers, and sung the loudest of everyone.

" Listen to the squawking coming from the windows" he would say as we passed

"These idiots should be honored to be in our presence," in a laughing tone only we could hear.

From 7:00 to 11:00 AM, and then from 1:00 to 5:00 PM it was drilling, calisthenics, and intense exercise and training on just about every feasible thing that we might encounter. This intense schedule culminated with our supper that was served until 7 PM, and from that time our time was our own. Most of us were so tired after those first few days that we were asleep before the 9 PM. lights out curfew that was never strictly enforced.

Many recruits were unable to keep up the pace of this exercise regime, and I saw few sort of falling by the wayside, unable to continue. I was in great shape, and was able to take everything that was dished out to me. I knew that this training was purposeful and meant to save my life, so I participated with all the effort I had. It would increase my stamina, and my ability to survive, so I never slacked off. I did suffer for the first few days with muscle soreness, as did everyone, but after the first week or so it became much easier.

As part of our training we were taught the mechanics of the Springfield rifle, the standard bolt action rifle of the day. We learned how to disassemble and clean the weapon and practiced shooting it on the firing ranges. I excelled in marksmanship along with a few others and we were then acknowledged as sharpshooters. This was most enjoyable and I felt at ease with a rifle.

Another facet of the training was our familiarization with and the use of the gasmask. We were taken to a hut that had been rigged to deploy this type of poison and were trained in operations while wearing the protective mask. Part of the training consisted of us removing the seal of our gasmask and experiencing the characteristics of this poison gas, and its effect on us.

They advised us to take a long deep breath when we had removed our protective gas masks.

These guys are crazy, and can go to hell I thought to myself, so I barely inhaled without the mask and was still able to experience the effects. That taste in my throat and the burning effect will always be remembered, and I immediately thought of the poor soldiers of World War I that were subjected to the horrible effects of Mustard Gas that was used during that period.

Joey, on the other hand took his mask off completely, and pretending he was breathing, turned to us crossing his eyes and made funny faces as if he were passing out. What a prankster, and he almost got into trouble with that stunt.

The government had taken over 90% of all the resorts in Miami for the use as training facilities. Just a few blocks from the hotel was a large golf course that had been transformed into our training field. This is where we would do calisthenics, learn marching in formation and do drill exercises.

After the first few days some resourceful soul made up a song that we all began to sing while doing cadence. It was about the Billows Hotel, that was rumored to have had somewhat of a jaded past. From brothel and speakeasy, this hotel was said to have had a comparable history of debauchery, similar to the goings-on in Havana, Cuba. While lawlessness and corruption were the norm in Cuba, southern Florida also had its share of similar goings on. Although never openly publicized, the Billows Hotel possessed that aura of mystique.

This made-up little ditty was sung to the tune of "The Caissons Go Rolling Along;" It went;

"Give a cheer, give a cheer for the boys that guzzle beer, in the cellars of Billows Hotel, They are strong, they are bold, it's a story seldom told, from the cellars of the Billows Hotel.

For it's guzzle, guzzle, guzzle as it trickles down the muzzle, squadron 13 ….. for e……ver, And we'll all give a cheer for the boys that guzzle beer, in the cellars of Billows Hotel."

It continued with three additional verses that progressively became a tad more risqué, at least by the standards of the forty's, but would be viewed clean when compared to the nonsense music of today.

Miami Beach was a resort town that I had only dreamed about. Most of its visitors prior to the war were affluent vacationers, relaxing on its white sandy beaches, sitting under palm trees, and swimming in the crystal clear waters. Beautiful pastel colored buildings dotted the streets, along with a constant breeze made this a far cry from what I had left at home. In the evenings, after dinner we were on our own and we were able to do almost anything we wanted. Most of us used this time for reading and writing letters from home, and resting after the strenuous military workouts from the day. Sundays were mostly rest days and there were no drill exercises so the majority of the day was spent cleaning our uniforms, polishing our shoes and getting caught up with the letters from home and relaxation.

There were also those card games that everyone seemed to get involved with on the off hours. We spent a lot of time playing poker, and Frankie and Joey were instrumental in showing me how to spot a cheat. They said they learned these techniques in south Philly where there was always some action of sorts going on. I left it at that, and learned the ins and outs of the game.

"How do you guys know so much about how these guys cheat" I asked in my naivety.

"Well, while you were born with that silver spoon in your mouth in Paterson, we here hustling any way we could. You know, we're the products of a miss-spent youth" they said laughingly.

The USO had facilities in Miami, and would always have something going on to keep us from getting homesick. They would host different activities and all types of entertainment for the troops. From movies to celebrity comedians there was always someone or something there to entertain us. The most well received of all the activities planned were the dances they sponsored. I don't know how or where they rounded up so many beautiful women, but there presence certainly uplifted our spirits.

The only problems were the competition from the officers, as they used their rank to try and impress the ladies. They had access to their exclusive club, and viewed themselves as superior. But you did the best you could.

I have to say was a little shy in the beginning, and spent most of the time on the sidelines along with most of the other young GI's. I began to notice that many other guys were dancing with all the girls and having great times, so I had myself a drink, from a flask that someone had smuggled into the dance and that loosened me up enough. I grabbed a beautiful lady and started dancing. I got into the swing of things, talked and laughed with some of the local women and had a wonderful time.

In 1943, Miami was not the booming metropolis of today. At the time, The Cadillac Hotel was the largest hotel there. It was seven stories high and was located on the corner of Lincoln and 50th street. From that point north, there was nothing but vast open land for miles, until the next town of Hollywood. Lincoln Avenue was the main road in Miami, and being adjacent to the ocean, it was subject to horrific storms, and with them came high winds. These winds blew with such ferocity that after the storms the road would be closed due to the sand dunes that accumulated on them. These inaccessible roads were then cleared by the Army, using bulldozers, and other heavy machinery.

There were vast open undeveloped expanses of shore line, patrolled by sailors, with attack dogs. I assume they were members of the Navy/Coast Guard, and their efforts were to keep our coast free of any covert operations threatening U.S. security. I still remember the pristine beauty of the area during my stay, it was truly paradise.

Chapter III

Continuation of Basic Training
Ground School Training
Gulfport, Mississippi

With the preliminary stages of our basic training completed in Miami, I was ordered to report to Gulfport, Mississippi for the next aspect of training.

Unfortunately, my buddies Frankie and Joey were given different orders and we said our goodbyes in Miami. It's sad, but I never heard from, nor saw Frankie or Joey again. I'm sure that if they survived, they now probably own South Philly. We had a great time together, and I hope all went well with them.

I was transported back to the train station, and boarded a train to my next destination. I sat with some friends, and we talked, and shared some stories of our escapades in Florida during the ride on that warm August afternoon of 1943. After hours of travel, we were told that we would be stopping for refueling in the depot at Mobile, Alabama. I watched as we pulled into the station, and commented to myself about the large size of a depot for the south, and the masses of switching rails, similar to the tracks you see entering Pennsylvania Station, NYC. Now these trains still used coal as fuel, and were steam powered throughout the south.

"Alright, everyone off the train," the conductor barked out. We were told that the stop would take about an hour, and we were free to disembark the train and stretch our legs.

It was a hot and humid day, but we had gotten used to that by now. There were hundreds of us in the rail yard, when out of the corner of my eye, I saw this young black kid, with a shoe-shine box strapped to his shoulder. He looked about ten years old, and a certain way about him as he asked the GI's if they wanted a shoe shine.

"Hey there mister GI, how bout a shine for dem dare boots of yo's" he said. He was a nice kid, obviously poor, as his clothes were tattered and wasn't even wearing shoes himself, but he had a certain way about him. He was just trying to make some money. He spoke with the traditional southern accent, and sort of bastardized the English language, but he had a big smile, and was polite as he asked if anyone wanted their shoes shined.

"I sho gives the best shoe shine in all ah Alabama," he said as he impishly frolicked, having procured a client for his service already and was putting on a sort of show, while snapping the polishing rag as he buffed the boots into a luster. He sang and bopped to the rhythm of his polishing, and there were a few soldiers lined up for a shine, sort of smiling at the entertainment.

Not bothering anyone, most of us sort of related to the kid, as during the depression most all of us did similar things to get by. But this kid had a certain charisma about him while making a few cents, most likely to help his family get by.

Out of the clear blue comes a railroad detective running full speed up behind this poor kid, screaming and cursing at him for annoying the GI's.

"Get your ass out of here" screamed the detective. "Haven't I warned you to stay the hell out-ah-here you !#$%^&!#$ bastard" as the poor kid, struggles to pick up his wares, staying well beyond the reaches of the detective.

"Hey, leave the kid alone" shouted a GI. "What the hell is wrong with you, you SOB"

"This is not your business," replied the rail detective.

"I'll show you what's my business" as a large man in uniform steps forward.

The youngster, obviously intimidated, was shaking with fear as he grabbed his box and began running out of the train yard. Unfortunately he had to pass in front of the detective as he made his way toward the exit, so to hasten his departure, the detective proceeded to kick this little kid as hard as he could in the backside.

"That's so you don't forget" barks the law officer, and I witnessed this poor kid catapulted at least two feet in the air from the force of this booting. The kid had wet himself and was crying and wincing in pain while he rubbed himself to ease the hurt.

Now there was trouble. The big man grabs the detective by the throat, and pins him to a wrought iron fence. Within seconds, a crowd of GI's, myself included gather, circling the detective and begin voicing outrage to what had just transpired.

"What the hell are you doing to that little kid" asked the big man as the detective squirmed, shocked at the intervention. At that point it wasn't a racial thing, it was purely moral. With a commotion stirring, a couple of black GI's pushed their way into the center of the disturbance, and said to the big man, that they would handle it.

"So you like to hit little kids," said one of the soldiers in a menacing tone, "How about trying that with me" as the verbal assault continued.

Next came the push......... than one big shove.......... and next the first big punch. Before you knew it, fists were flying, the crowd was roaring as we all closed in, and the detective seemed to be taking the worst of it. Everyone crowded around to get a better view, as punches were exchanged, teeth were being spit out, and the blood was flowing.

This was the most excitement that had happened in days, as punch after punch was thrown; there were knock downs, grunts and groans as they continued. It's unfortunate, that the cause of this incident was sheer ignorance and racial prejudice.

Within seconds, whistles were blowing, and the MP's were intervening, pushing their way into the crowd, trying to restore order. As they broke up the fight, and proceeded to appease the crowd to avoid a potential riot, we were all forced back onto the train.

14

I'm sure the MP's handled this in a more appropriate manner than the local law enforcement would have, and due to racial conditions in the south at the time, I'm glad they did. The railroad detective was clearly wrong for using such aggressive force against this poor kid who was doing nothing but trying to make some pocket change. It was really sad to see how things actually were in the south during that era. We all spoke in behalf of the intervening soldiers who came to the rescue of the shoeshine boy, and while I am sure that they were brought up on charges, hopefully they were dismissed when the circumstances were revealed. We all felt that the soldiers were justified in reacting to the situation, and although their reaction was more of an emotional reaction to social behavior in that part of the country, it was warranted considering the circumstances.

For the balance of our time in Alabama, we were forced back on the train, the railroad made a conscious effort to get us the hell out of there in a timely fashion. I think they viewed us as trouble makers, threatening the balance of power in the south. Due to this episode our refueling was moved to top priority, and we quickly departed the station, within ten minutes of the incident.

As luck would have it, the big man sat down in the same car, so I took the opportunity to introduce myself.

"Hey, that was a good thing you did out there" I said to the big man, "my name is Nick" as I held out my hand.

"Thanks, Salvatore," he replied, shaking my hand. "Sal Capolla."

I had seen Salvatore before, during basic training in Miami, but had never befriended him.

Sal was one of those guys that were unable to keep up with the exercise regime during our initial phase of basic training. He looked much slimmer than the first time I had seen him, but was still a very large man.

"It's terrible what that guy did to that little shoe-shine boy" I said.

"I just hate anyone who picks on little kids" he replied.

"Oh there you are, I thought you were going to be arrested by the MP's" interjects a stranger.

"Nah"... replies Sal, "Hey Nino, meet Nick"

I introduced myself, and the three of us began talking.

Salvatore was born and raised in Worcester, Massachusetts, and Nino, born in Italy, resided in Brooklyn N.Y.

Nino spoke with a distinct accent, but not to the point that made him difficult to understand. The train pulls away from the station as we continue our conversation which included a full commentary, and highlights of the fight.

We are constantly interrupted by fellow service men that had witnessed Salvatore's intervention, as they acknowledged his intentions, patting him on the back.

For the duration of the trip we engaged in conversation while partaking in the traditional entertainment of nickel a hand Poker. We rode for hours until reaching our destination, and pulled into the station around dusk. We were all tired from the trip, but still a little hopped up from the melee.

Gulfport Mississippi was a nice southern town that seems to have exploded as a result of the military bases located there. We settled in to our new home and hit the ground running. We were on a rigorous training schedule during the next five months that included intensive ground studies; learning the fundamentals of the Curtis-Wright Aircraft engines between our regular drilling, calisthenics, and marching exercises.

This engine was cylindrical and had eighteen pistons, nine in the front and nine in the back. We were taught to assemble and disassemble this engine and taught how to repair this type of aircraft engine. This engine was to be the one that would power the new B-29 Superfortress that I would be assigned to.

Classroom instructors varied, and many were civilians that also included the fairer sex.

I was blessed to have my buddies Sal, and Nino in some classes, as we had all become good friends. Teaching us one facet of the mechanical aspect of our training, was a beautiful blonde that spoke with a southern accent that drove the men crazy. Elvira was her name, and she was the talk of the group. She had the right stuff all right, and I'm sure she knew it. Everyone tried to move her, and I think that she had heard every line in the book.

"Now you boys need to fully understand the material before we can move on, now are there any questions" she would say, as some nincompoop from the back would shout some crude response.

Now Elvira was no dumb blonde and that's where most men went wrong. She was educated, far more so than anyone in her class. It was rumored that her fiancé was a lieutenant that had been shipped off to Europe, and hadn't written for a while. Some friends had told her of his Lotharios antics in England, so as a result all the eligible young men on base that had heard, thought they had a shot at her. When she walked, and she did so in the most provocative manner, there were enlisted mens eyes following her every beat. It was like poetry in motion as she would swing and sway down the hall ways.

Now Elvira wasn't the only young female instructor, there were many more and human nature being what it was, most men were competing for the ladies affections. One instance in particular that I recall was that of this young southern soldier, Hicks.

Now Hicks was an Alabama boy who thought that he had what it took to get a date with one of the female instructors, but had a little problem with personal hygiene.

"Y'all yank's don't know how to romance a fine southern belle like that, I'll show you how it's done" he said

"If that stinking SOB gets a date with anything, it should be with a shower" Nino commented.

It was hot and humid in Gulfport and old Hicks certainly was foul smelling. He hadn't changed his fatigues for days, they were full of sweat, and he reeked.

A few discrete comments were made to him, to no avail, and the next day this guy had the same cloths on again, and was smelling putrid. It was obvious the diplomatic approach had not worked, and he was nauseating to be around.

Drastic measures therefore had to be taken because the stench became unbearable.

After class, while Hicks was sucking up to the instructor, Salvatore grabbed Old Stinky, threw him outside into a make shift shower, clothes and all. Nino had grabbed a fire hose and began spraying him, knocking him down from the pressure. I had procured large wooden pot scrubbers that I had borrowed from the mess hall. As the group took turns throwing soap on him, others were scrubbing him with the industrial sized scrubbers. We all laughed as we hosed him down, as he gasped for air.

"Hicks, you can't impress the ladies when you smell like a horses ass, even if you are a fine southern gentleman,' Sal yells out laughingly from the crowd.

While the incident was forgotten in a few days, Old Stinky seemed to have learned a valuable lesson, and never suffered from that type of problem again, or should I say we never suffered from that sort of problem through out our training. Ultimately, Hicks became good friends with all of us, I'm sure that this was done primarily to change his superior disposition of how to attract females, But I never found out if he landed a date with the instructor.

We had all been taught self defense techniques as part of basic training, and I, along with a few others, were singled out for having some potential for boxing.

The first time I had gloves on I was matched to Murphy, a burly Irishman who outweighed me by at least 20 pounds.

"Come on you big SOB" I said taunting him as I threw the first punch "lets go" I said while peppering him back and forth.

"Stand still you little chicken" Murphy responded.

"You got nothing" I replied as I danced around everything thrown at me.

I knew that if I stopped, Murphy would clock me, so I moved around the ring until the bell sounded.

"I like what I saw out there" said the instructor after the match. "Murphy didn't't touch you, that's good footwork" he continued, so at that that point I was slated to represent our outfit in the weight class.

Between classes and calisthenics the boxing instructors taught me some additional principles in the art, and built up my confidence. As with all men in their early twenties, we are under the impression that we are invincible and very impressionable as to what the trainer fills your head with. He convinces you of a natural ability that you have been gifted with, and stresses that it would be a shame to waste such a talent. After some training and encouragement I agreed to try a bout against another GI in my weight class. I was a strapping 118 pounds at the time and thought I was in good shape. I guess at the weight this would be the equivalent of a feather weight class in today's boxing, or maybe even ultra-feather weight as I look back at some of my photos of the time. It seems that I had not one ounce of fat on me at the time but not much meat on my bones either.

Anyway, these were only one round bouts, similar to the Golden Gloves. These bouts were more for the entertainment of the enlisted men, and were basically a form of competition between other outfits. The ring was set up in the indoor training area and seats were placed all around the ring so all the GI's could watch the fights. This rivalry drew large crowds of enlisted men to these matches not exclusively for the sport of the entertainment but mostly to place friendly wagers on the outcome of the events.

I enjoyed the popularity of representing our outfit, and became friendly with most of the guys in our group. They tried to give me advice, and since we all trained in the same area I knew most of the other guys that would be my rivals

17

There were always questions on the opponents we were to face, and friends would try to get a feeling for how we felt before the bout.

"Hey Nick, how you feel about Stevens, have you seen his technique" asked one in my group.

"Yea, he's sort of a straight on approach kind of guy, no real finesse" I replied.

"How about Shultz, I hear that bastard is strong" came another question.

"He sure is, I'm glad he's in another weight class" I replied.

I guess they shared the information with the camp in determining what odds would be given for the betting. There was a sort of hierarchy within the camp that had an inside track in knowing who would fight who before everyone else had the information. It was an exciting week or so leading up to the event and from my recollection there were to be about 25 of these mini-bouts on this day.

I recall entering the ring to the cheers of my group and being given my last minute instructions by the trainer.

"Stay away from him, jab and move. Just keep sticking and moving" my trainer said.

I nodded, "he's always open on the left side, so take advantage of that" he repeated.

After sharing with me what he felt were the weaknesses of my opponent, I nodded in acknowledgment and entered the ring. I remember the gong of the bell and the cheers of the spectators as we made our way to the center of the ring.

I sized him up for a few seconds, then saw an opening and launched a left jab at him, a short shot to the head. It got through and landed on its mark as I saw him take a step backwards. Feeling more confident now I tried again throwing another left jab to his bobbing head and connected again square in the jaw. I recall hearing howling cheers from the crowd, so I set up again and threw a combination left and right, then took a step back and waited. As my opponent approached me, I threw a left to the body followed by an uppercut that hit him square on the button.

OK, this guys knees buckled, He's ready to go down I thought.

Well he certainly was dazed, and I hadn't broken a sweat yet. The fight had been going for at least a minute and I was doing surprisingly well.

Maybe the instructor was right in saying that I showed promise in boxing I said to myself.

My opponent seemed unable to land a blow on me as I deflected everything he threw at me. Feeling really confident at this time I threw a big right at him, while regrettably dropping my left and I was tagged a hard shot to the noggin. I backed up a step, momentarily dazed from the impact of the punch, shook my head and I swear I saw those little birdies flying around my head, tweet-tweeting for a few seconds. Fighting the impulse to stare up at the birds, I regained my composure and spent the rest of the fight with a less aggressive attitude. I certainly was glad when the bell rang and the fight was over. I don't recall the outcome of that fight, neither of us was knocked down, but we both gave each other some good shots. There were no head protectors in use then as there are today in amateur boxing.

After that first bout, the instructor gave me encouragement about how well I had done, and asked if I wanted to continue in place advancement for the next day. I thought for a while and determined that I was not meant for boxing. Something about being whacked in the head didn't't seem to agree with me. Maybe it was the headache I had just gotten, seeing those little birdies flying around my head, or the thought of my brains being pounded into scrambled eggs and for what? The Army had taught us to defend ourselves as a means of survival, and I was never the aggressive tough guy type. The thought of giving someone a shellacking, or for that matter taking one, didn't't sound all that appealing to me. I found it more enjoyable watching the fights from outside the ring, and after all, being a spectator to a boxing match had its advantages. One being, you didn't't need to take aspirin for the headaches afterwards.

Always looking for something to occupy our spare time we would always try to find some recreational activities to do on our down time. Now Mississippi in the 40's was rural and being young men away from home with cash in our pockets we were game for most anything. Now outside from the obvious, I recall hearing about a little place on the outskirts of town that rented horses. This sounded like a fun way to spend an afternoon so a group of us got together to go horseback riding.

This place was way out of town and took us a very long time to get there. We traveled by bus and as we disembarked, it reminded me of taking a trip down Tobacco Road. As we walked past the shack that I think housed this family, I couldn't't help but notice the small tribe of children frolicking around. There were six or seven of these half naked imps that I saw, running and jumping everywhere like wild Indians, and not a one wearing shoes. As we approached a rickety building and corral, a pregnant woman, also barefoot smiled at us from her clothes line. The hand painted sign advertising the place had a misspelled word or two, but who cared? The proprietor greeted us with a smile that was missing a few teeth. He sure was a Good Old Boy, the kind you know had a still out back making corn liquor or Moonshine Whiskey, what we would call a Hillbilly.

We spoke for a while, and began haggling over the price for our party. I initiated this, trying to get a discounted price, and told the owner that we had connections for getting more GI's to his establishment. However, before we were able to recommend his establishment he would have to prove to us that the establishment warranted us doing so.

When I was satisfied with everything, I would advertise his establishment on the base.

"You know that there are seven of us here today, and a few thousand of us back at the base" I said to him. "With me spreading the word about your place, you're going to be making a whole lot of money."

This weathered old codger listened to me intently, staring me dead in the eye as I spoke. He nodded his head and occasionally rubbed his chin whiskers over what appeared to be three days worth of stubble. He lifted his sweat stained hat and scratched his head, while shooing flies from his head as I continued with my pitch to him.

"Are all those kids yours," I asked him

"Shoot, I got five more a-doin chores out back" he replied.

"You know, this is how all business is done back home, and after I promote this place, there would be hordes of people lined up to pay your price" I said,

"You'll be making so much money that you'll need to hire on more people."

"Where you from anyway boy" asked the proprietor of me, "Cause you sure talk kinda fast...., and smooth,......you one of them Yankee boys, ain't you?"

I replied in my best interpretation of a southern accent. "Shoot, I ain't no Yankee, matter of fact, I'm from the south....... South Jersey that is," as my colleagues burst out laughing.

The owner smirked at me, and obviously failed to see the humor, nodded and said

"Well boys, tell ya'll what I'm goin do............. Mr. Yankee, I like your style and I'm a-gonna take special care ah you today." Even though the agreed upon price was negligble, we all had some fun with the old timer.

Since there were seven of us in the group, and only five horses saddled, most of the guys in our group had already picked their horses, and were mounted. As I waited for the other horses to be brought out to us, the others set off down the path where they would wait for us. A single horse was brought out and as I approached it, one of the hands told me not to take this horse, that mine was coming out shortly. Nino mounted the horse, and began in a leisurely pace to meet with the others that were still in sight. Everyone had taken off guiding their horses in the direction they wanted. Everyone, that is but me.

As I waited, this beautiful highly spirited horse is brought out to me, a spotted Appaloosa that was even giving trouble to the hand that had brought him out. The horse bucked and kicked, and reared on its hind legs as it neared me. I was told to hop on him, and proceeded to make an attempt, but the animal reared and seemed determined to not have anyone mount him. I backed off, and saw the proprietor sort of laughing from afar.

"Hey old timer, what's going on, are you running out of horses" voicing my displeasure at his choice of horse for me, and he quickly gave the hand orders to bring out another horse.

Now this next animal was a beautiful horse, sort of a Chestnut Brown in color and seemed to have a better demeanor than the first one. I immediately hopped on, and grabbed the reins and jabbed the horse to get going so I could catch up with the others, but the horse wouldn't't move. I prodded its side haunches with my boots again, but still nothing. I did it a little harder, again with no reaction. I spoke while urging on the horse, "Giddy Up," but failed to get any response. By this time my buddies had made enough progress down the road that they were almost gone from sight. I was becoming frustrated, and thought to myself that the owner had deliberately given me difficult horses. I called out for some help, as I had become annoyed with the situation. I turned looking for assistance, and out of the corner of my eye I saw someone coming to my aid, or so I thought. He must have been twenty feet away when I heard this whirling sound, and in a nanosecond I heard the crack of a whip behind me. My horse reared up and we were off like a rocket.

I was holding on for dear life as this horse put me through the paces, running wildly out of control. Passing my group of buddies, they looked in astonishment as I flew by them along the forested trail. They said later that they had no idea that I was such an experienced rider as I quickly disappeared in a cloud of dust into the underbrush. Obviously they hadn't noticed the panicked look on my face. There were branches that I had to duck under, tree trunks that I had to maneuver around, all while trying to keep balanced and on top of this deranged animal. Now this animal wanted no part of me being on his back either, as he jerked and reared incessantly, even once slowed quickly, and bucked in an effort to throw me off. We came to a rock wall that

20

seemed like the end of the line, or so I thought. With a great stride the horse leaped over the stone wall, and I held onto the horn while air born. I was trying to lean in the direction of travel with the horse, but the animal sensed this and turned sharply in the other direction in another attempt to throw me. I made every possible effort to stay on him until finally the horse tired and began slowing down, thank God.

Well I jumped off the horse, as I had certainly had my fill of riding and I walked back to return the horse and to speak my mind to the owner.

I had about a 15 minute walk to get back to the corral, and I was seething every step of the way. When I finally saw him, I was primed and lit into him verbally for being so thoughtless in his actions, especially for whipping the animal that way with a rider on it.

"What the hell is the matter with you, you crazy old SOB. Why did you whip the horse like that" I asked.

This simpleton sat there laughing hysterically holding his belly, and turning red in the face, occasionally coughing from lack of breath. He had been chomping on the end of a cigar that he almost swallowed in one of the gasps of air between laughs. His eyes bulged, as he tried to spit out the stogie, while half choking, eyes tearing trying to catch his breath. This guy was laughing so hard that I began to laugh just watching him.

Semi gaining his composure, and after taking a deep breath, he nodded his head, he said something like,

"Well son you didn't't tell me you couldn't't ride" with that toothless smile and that southern drawl. "I thought you Yankee boys knew bout horses," as he burst out in another fit of uncontrollable laughter, as his face turned a reddish-blue hue of crimson.

"I guess all you business men from up north ain't got much horse sense," as yet another round of hysterical laughter erupted.

It seems, as I was to find out later that I was not the first one to try to capitalize on the premise of advertising this facility to the base. I thought that I could finesse this country bumpkin, but as it turned out he hoodwinked me. I was told later on that every new group of soldiers stationed in Mississippi had tried some sort of angle with him. Well, you live and learn, and I guess you couldn't be mad at those southern boys for still harboring a grudge against us Yankees from, I guess as long ago as the Civil War. Needless to say my friends all had a great laugh at my expense, they spoke of this look on my face as I streaked pass them.

I was somewhat battered and bruised from the experience, and spent the entire bus trip back to the base removing burrs from under my clothing, and nursing the cuts and lacerations I had suffered.

I woke up the next morning stiff as a board, but loosened up after our morning workout. The whole barracks had heard about our little escapade while horseback riding and I was chidingly asked to go with another group to help negotiate the price.

We all laughed about it for a while, and it seems that everyone on the base had heard the story, so I was teased about it for a few days. So as a result for the remainder of the time in Mississippi I learned to stay with the more traditionally conservative forms of weekend entertainment. The movie theater in town, the occasional dance, or show by the USO, or having a few beers with the boys at the PX. The beer they served us in the PX was Near-Beer, of the 3.2 variety and never succeeded in doing anything much but creating a long line to the toilet. No one had a car, so transportation was by bus, or train and television hadn't entered the picture yet. (No pun intended).

We were given additional training in marksmanship during our stay in Gulfport. Our entire group was marched to the firing ranges for orientation. We started with some brief instruction of firearms, as to how they were to be handled, and the safety aspects. The instructor was the philosophy that learning by doing was the best teacher, so he showed us what to do once then hand out the firearms. I had fired the bolt action rifles in Florida and was confident in my abilities in marksmanship, but as I was to find out these were not rifles but shot guns. The object of this exercise was to hit the flying puck, the equivalent of skeet shooting today. You would get acclimated to the weight and feel of the weapon, then call out for the puck that would be launched into your range of fire from a cement building on the range. The objective was obviously to take aim and destroy the moving puck. After my first shot, the shotgun recoiled to the extent that it almost knocked me to the ground. I was skin and bone and felt like my shoulder was dislocated. The smiling instructor suggested folding a towel in an attempt to cushion the recoil against my shoulder. It did make things somewhat better, but I still ended up black and blue on my entire shoulder.

Gunnery training consisted of every possible exercise as a means to enhancing our abilities to hit moving targets. We were loaded individually on flatbed trucks and driven at fast speeds through the shooting range as clay pigeons were launched at us and we were expected to hit them. As time progressed I became a great shot and learned the principles of leading the target to score a hit. On occasion someone would miss and the clay pigeons would hit the trucks or worse yet hit the shooter.

Our training also included machine guns similar to the ones we would be using on the aircraft. These were also large caliber machine guns mounted onto military jeeps that we were taught to become proficient in hitting targets while moving. On the pistol range I also excelled and felt very at ease with marksmanship. While pistols were easier to control even though they were 45 calibers, the recoil went up instead of back. I became a Marksman with all weapons after a sort, and received awards for my marksmanship abilities.

For the last two weeks of our training in Mississippi, we were taken into the near forest where we learned wilderness survival techniques. We slept in tents and were shown strategies meant to keep us alive if we were ever faced with this type of situation. This included how to build a basic structure to keep warm, find water, and even live off the land. It also included tips for finding direction and making it back to the Allied lines. This was great and the first time I had ever slept outdoors, or experienced sleeping under the stars. Most of us there had come from large cities and had never done this type of camping. I think most of us lost sight of what this exercise was really about and enjoyed the change of pace and scenery. Again, youth being what it is, there was a tendency to overlook the seriousness of this type of survival training. I thank God I was fortunate enough never to be forced to rely on that training for my survival. I guess that just goes to show how naive we really were.

Saying goodbye to Gulfport was not that easy as I had made some great friends and shared some wonderful times. Elvira, still was the talk of the base, had somehow moved to second fiddle when the USO showgirls were in town. It just so happened that our last night in Gulfport, a show was put on with Bob Hope, and some pin-up girls, performing on a makeshift stage close to the airplane hangars. That was a great send off.

Chapter IV

Long Beach, California

The next day, bright and early we were on the move again. It was January of 1944 and but of course we were in day coaches on a train heading cross country to Long Beach, California. This was a long grueling trip in those days. For days we traveled again in those uncomfortable day coaches in our trek to the west coast. We passed through the desert with not much to see, but again passed the time by honing our skills in the art of Poker playing.

Upon arrival I noticed how beautiful things were in this part of the country. There was bright sunshine, temperate climate and no humidity. It was January and back east we would be knee deep in slush and snow. Here however it was comfortable without even a jacket on, so as far as I was concerned it didn't't get much better than that.

We were stationed in barracks very close to the Douglas Air Craft Factory and we attended classes there, and it was much the same regime as the other bases we had attended. There were classes on various aspects of mechanical and physical properties of large planes as well as similarities of all types of warplanes. Basically we ran the gambit on what made them tick. We learned the physics of flight and aerodynamics. There were also classes on design feature showing both the strengths and weaknesses of all planes. This included the German design war birds, and of much greater interest to us, were the Japanese planes that we would be up against in the field.

Weaknesses in the enemies' aircraft are advantageous to learn especially knowing that we would be defending ourselves against these very aircrafts. Attacking the most vulnerable point of the enemies' plane gave you a tactical and strategic advantage. The Zeros Achilles heel was their fuel tanks, and they had extreme difficulties with the self-sealing function of their tanks. As a result, when hit their fuel tanks would spew its contents and hopefully flame the plane. I was thrilled to be learning about the design features of the enemies air craft, with design drafting having been my occupation prior to my being drafted. We also were privileged enough to see the huge assembly facilities at Douglas plant, and see first hand the people that were actually building these planes.

On one of our daily visits to the facility, I recall seeing the assembly of the C-47's. These were cargo planes that were also used as troop transports. As far as the eye could see there was nothing but these crafts. They were mostly being assembled by women. All facets of the population were doing their part in aiding the war effort. That's what made this country so great both then, and now. I think the enemy greatly underestimated the American mind set and work ethic both in our labor force and spirit. By assuming that American women were too delicate to fill this manufacturing void was a miss calculation that cost the enemy the war. I would like to acknowledge all these civilians, both men and women that rose to the occasion, tackling these difficult jobs that had historically been done mostly by men. Acknowledgment, however is not enough, I want to thank them with all of my heart for their accomplishments. They not only did the job, but they did it well. I take my hat off to these wonderful people who supplied us with the tools on the home front needed to win the war. They truly are the heroes, the unseen, and unacknowledged, but never the less their importance was critical in the outcome of the war.

Our training in Long Beach continued in much the same way as our training in Gulfport. We were still doing marching drills and heavy calisthenics we were still kept busy every waking moment of the day.

The California weather as I said earlier was wonderful with bright sunshine and the orange groves that seemed to be everywhere were beautiful. As a result, we all looked forward to the forthcoming passes to go into town to blow off a little steam. I recall one particular instance while stationed in Long Beach that we all had become antsy, and were given a pass for the day. There were trolleys close to the base, so on this sunny afternoon a group of us hopped a ride and went to the Long Beach Amusement Pier just to have some fun. It seemed like the perfect place to forget about the war and all the training we were being given to fight in it, so we were all just relieved to spend a day away from the base and the routine.

As soon as we arrived this wave of depression came over me. I don't recall what triggered this, maybe it was seeing some families spending time together, or the thought of us soon being shipped overseas but I just became so homesick that I felt that I had to leave. I guess it was some sort of anxiety in my psyche, but I just felt like I had to see my family, immediately that I almost felt like going AWOL. My friends, noticing my emotional state immediately took control of the situation. It's funny how your buddies become your support group and like an extended family, a brotherhood, we all tried to help each other.

"Hey Nick, what's wrong" asked Smitty.

"I don't know, I've just got this bad feeling, like I've got to get out of here" I replied.

"My heart is pounding a mile a minute, I think….I think…..I've got to get back to my family, I can't, I can't"

I had stopped and sat at a bench.

"Come on man, the feeling will pass" Smitty reassured me.

"You've just got a case of the blues, and I know the remedy for it" he said.

The guys got me up and about and kept me thinking right until the depression passed. I later thanked them as they replied don't worry about it. The rest of the day we spent having fun by playing pinball machines and winning prizes along the pier. We also talked to lovely young ladies that we met along the way. Everyone was so warm and friendly to us that I never had a second thought of my family or the depression that had overcome me earlier. It's funny how fragile our psyche is and what effects us. We ended up in a nice Cocktail lounge that evening talking to some local lovelies and it seems that was just what the doctor ordered for me. Old Smitty was right, he knew the sure fire remedy for the blues, female companionship.

I recall having a drink, than another, and I think one after that and felt great. I was talking away to whomever, and recall spending time with this young lady at the bar. The company was wonderful, and the drinks were flowing, it doesn't't get any better than that. We got back to the barracks late and hit the sack immediately.

I woke up the next morning with a slight headache, and in my pockets were two girls' addresses. It wasn't my hand writing, as far as I knew, or could I remember, as I pondered back on the vague memories of the evening before, I think I had a good time.

The crew that I was out with filled me in on some of the vague details of the previous evening while we were having breakfast, and laughingly commented on my maneuvering the ladies. We all had a good time, and it seemed that blowing off some steam like that is a necessary release from reality.

I had heard of the beautiful beaches in southern California, but unfortunately the winter season is not conducive to swimming in California, as it is in Florida, so one of our cronies suggested a trip to Tijuana, Mexico for our first weekend pass. There were rumors about a bar there that highlighted a girl that put on a show. It involved the girl, a donkey and a bottle of tequila, and oh well........... the rest was so bizarre that upon hearing it, you just have to laugh. From what we had heard there was just about lawlessness in the border town, and to tell the truth, I was apprehensive about going there.

To my good fortune, or not, I never had a chance to visit Mexico, or to find out first hand of the legend of the girl from Tijuana. However, I think that same rumor still exists today.

I also have fond memories of my stay there. While Long Beach was mostly an agricultural area at the time, excluding the military facilities, and seaport I thought that it would be a wonderful place to live and seriously thought about it returning to California after the war. We were in Long Beach till May, 1944.

Chapter V

Clovis, New Mexico

We were then sent, again by train, to Clovis Air Force base in Clovis, New Mexico. We would remain there through October of the same year. Here at Clovis we began hands-on training learned techniques of aerial bombing and gunnery practices in the B-17, the standard bomber aircraft of the day. At about that time we began hearing talk of a newer and larger aircraft that was soon to be arriving at our base and a few months later, the B-29 SUPERFORTRESS did arrive.

I was in total awe upon first sight of it, as I gazed open-mouthed at its magnificence and splendor. It was unlike anything I had ever seen, and for a few minutes I just gazed in astonishment at its size. There was an old B-17 that we had been using for training purposes parked on the hard stand next to the new Superfort, and it was approximately two and a half times the size of the B17, and dwarfed it by comparison.

I took one look at this monster and said, "I'm sure glad that this thing is on our side." This bomber had the look of a ferocious predator asleep on the hard stand. It reminded me of a flying dragon, poised and ready to pounce. It growled to life upon ignition, snarling, seemingly ready to devour its opposition.

"This is the dragon that will rain hell on Japan" I said silently.

There were massive four-bladed propellers powered by four Curtis-Wright engines that were made in Paterson, N.J. my home-town, and the plane had a totally new concept for its landing gear. Instead of using the wheel configuration side and tail as was on the B-17, the B-29 had a front and side wheel configuration tricycle type landing gear. This design feature was unique for its time, and obviously had merit for it is still in operational use today. At 99 feet long and a little over 27 feet high, with a wing span of 141 feet, this silver bullet would utilize an 11-man crew to make it come to life. And the best part was that I was being trained to be a part of that crew.

Other new innovations were introduced on the B-29 such as pressurized cabin zones, designed to eliminate the need for oxygen masks while flying at high altitudes. This too eliminated the feared Aviators Bends, a phenomenon that affects flyers that creates the formation of nitrogen bubbles in the blood. This happened at altitudes in excess of 10,000 feet, when it was necessary to breathe from oxygen canisters for extended periods of time, and results from changes in altitude that occur too quickly. Deep sea divers also suffered a similar malady known as decompression sickness or the Bends.

The new pressurized feature allowed us to fly at a much higher altitude than its predecessor, and at this height, theoretically no anti-aircraft guns could reach it, making it much safer than B-17.

The guns that would be under my control were now computer controlled and electronically fired from a remote location. This meant that a gunner would no longer stand behind the machine gun, and physically shoot. Instead, he would sit in a separate compartment behind the wings next to the Plexiglas blisters where our trigger mode was located. This was an area that housed the machinery needed to aim at a target.

On the screen were our gun sights that had cross hairs in a circle, and this new system took some getting used to, as aiming became an exercise in coordination and dexterity. These were computer type screens that images were viewed via a type of periscope, and in the beginning I found it difficult getting a proper sense of perception. Once you spotted the enemy you would track it, on the screen using long flowing motions keeping it within the parameter of the outline. With two handles you kept the target in place, as the computer measured wing span within the reticle (circle of dots) and calculated distance, rate of closure, and trajectory in your circle of cross hairs. This primitive computer was capable of calculating wind velocity, air speed, and every other possible variable that could affect the probability of hitting the target. The key to success was in the tracking, and in keeping either the wing span, or the body of the plane within the circle of dots long enough for the computer to set up. If all was calculated properly you then fired your guns with deadly accuracy. The weapons were located above and below the plane housed in rotating turrets that sheltered two fifty caliber machine guns per turret. These rotating turrets were designed remotely in a manner as not to compromise the pressurization of the aircraft. As a result, the gunner who had the best shot would fire at the enemy from as many as three separate locations at the same time. That would be three separate guns at different angles converging on one target.

The tail gunner sat alone in the back of the plane and was in charge of two fifty caliber machine guns. To add a little more sting to the enemy he also controlled a twenty millimeter cannon that had the capability of blowing the enemy fighters out of the sky. This position was the only one on the plane that the operator had full manual control of what he was shooting at.

The range of the B-29 was far superior to anything that had ever been built. Every conceivable method of reducing drag was implemented to achieve this. The rivets that held the plane together were counter-sunk giving this plane a flatter, sleeker appearance contributing to its aerodynamics. Weight always being a consideration in efficiency and its effect on consumption of fuel to maximize flying range, these planes were unpainted in an effort to lighten the load. This plane was designed specifically for one purpose to take the war to the Japanese Empire the mainland and we were being trained to administer this air powered assault.

The months through October 31st 1944 we were training exclusively in this beautiful new aircraft. We, as a crew, were expected to learn every nuance of this new bomber and to become proficient at every facet of delivering the devastation to the enemy that this bomber was designed and produced to do.

Our original crew's lineup began as follows; in the front compartment sat our pilot Second Lt. William Wills, 23 year-old from Washington State. The co-pilot was Second Lt. Ronald Bowerman, 19, from Oregon. Along with them sat the bombardier, Second Lt. James Alexander, 27, from Arkansas, navigator Second Lt. Arthur Stafford, 20, from Oklahoma. Also stationed in the front compartment was the radio operator, Corporal Eugene French, 23, from Illinois, and Staff Sergeant Engineer, John Baldasty, 30 from Washington State. Proceeding front to rear next sat radar gunner Corporal Gaylord Rice, 27, from Iowa, fire control Corporal James Shepard, 18, from Indiana, left blister gunner Corporal Billy Frazier, 20, from Texas and me, right blister gunner, Corporal Nick Constandelis, 22, from New Jersey. Alone in the rear compartment sat the tail gunner, Sergeant James Robinson, 23, from Ohio.

Connecting the front and rear pressurized compartments was a tunnel, or crawl space about three feet in diameter. This tube was routed over the two bomb bays and was padded with a type of matting that looked like the blankets that the moving men use to cover furniture. The crew would crawl through to access the front of the plane whenever the situation warranted us being there. Any communication within the plane, especially to the front while flying would be done with the use of the intercom system at the press of a button. For example, I would press the button on the intercom saying, "Right blister gunner to radio operator, over." He would then use his intercom and acknowledge the call and we would talk. We were becoming more and more at ease with flying together and maneuvering this giant behemoth as our training schedule had us flying daily, familiarizing us with the new bomber.

During out stay in Clovis we would receive the occasional passes to town, to blow off some steam. I had met some new friends while stationed here, but Nino and Sal had also made the move, and still remained my closest pals, and they accompanied the group on many leaves.

Nino was a tall, thin kid that spoke with the slightest accent, but was nevertheless very gregarious. He just loved to talk about anything. I think he had 11 siblings, of which he was somewhere in the middle, that might be the reason for his constant babbling. We had become very good friends, and shared much in common.

Nino also had a way about him when it came to the ladies, you know the type, always knowing what to say, and when to say it. He would always comment about Clovis,

"All we see ova-here is cowboys, and the ladies … maron-ami,…. they look-a-like-a men too. Hey Nick, you eva see such a place like this. I see this one lady in town one time, she look-a like-a horse, I'm a-tell you. I looked for a saddle on her back, I don't a-understand this-a place."

Needless to say Nino's commentary always had me laughing.

On one occasion, a group of us decided to go into the town of Clovis just to see what it was like. The day was spent looking around, as this was a small western town in 1944. We saw a restaurant, and Salvatore, recommended it as Great so we all stopped in for dinner.

Now Salvatore, being a large man, loved to eat, and I'm sure he researched the few eateries in the town. If anyone would know where a good place to eat was, it was Sal, so we followed his lead.

We all, piled into the establishment and naturally Nino begins talking to the waitress about her being the most attractive lady he's seen since he has been in Clovis.

His flirting had her smiling, blushing from all the attention, as we all placed the same orders for steaks, fries, and beer.

After about 15 minutes or so, the waitress comes out with these 13" oval plates and served us these jumbo T-bone steaks that were so large that they overlapped the sides of the plate. I just had to look at the plate and I became full.

I had the good fortune of having Nino on one side, and Salvatore on the other, and Salvatore dug into his meal like it was his last on this earth. His knife and fork were moving so quickly, I thought I saw sparks coming from the utensils. I kept my hands out of the way for fear that he might slip, and they too might also be devoured.

"I don't understand why they don't have spaghetti here, I just love spaghetti, It just doesn't't seem like a meal if I don't have it" Salvatore comments.

Astonishingly, a look down at his plate revealed a devoured meal, a bare bone, clean of any remnants of meat, as he grabs a hunk of bread to sop up any remaining juices.

"Are you still hungry" I ask Sal, as I see him eyeing my plate.

"Are you done ... well, if you're done,... I wouldn't't want it to go to waste" he replies sliding my barely eaten steak in front of him.

I felt bloated on the small portion I had eaten, and watched Salvatore completely put away my steak.

"Hey Salvatore, you full yet" questions Nino, as he waves to get the waitress's attention.

Having completed our meal, our stomachs bloated, we each received our bill for a grand total of $1.00 per meal, including the beer! The south west was a large beef producing area in America during that time, but that was still cheap.

Sal instantly became my seating partner, and the three of us were almost inseparable. We would revisit that place frequently and always had a ball in doing so. I became very popular with seating arrangements on these outings, due largely to the fact of the size portions I consumed and my generosity with the leftovers. I usually ended up passing on three quarters of the steak and gave to anyone interested, but Sal usually had the balance of my portion.

On our first full weeks pass, our group decided to go further into Texas to do some sight seeing. We hopped a bus to Lubbock, Texas and saw some sights and relaxed for a while. I guess we were in the outskirts of the town and it seemed typically rural and old fashion, like most of the small towns in the United States. With not much else to do, most of the guys frequented the local saloon and would have some fun getting drunk. This was never my idea of having fun, as I really wasn't that much of a drinker. I did however accompany the guys to a bar one evening for lack of something better to do. Now here we were in Texas, in a cowboy bar, where they still had places to tie up your horses outside the bar. The people were sort of friendly, but let's face it, we were the outsiders there. We all wore our uniforms and these folks still dressed in blue jeans and wore large ten gallon hats.

On this particular night, most of us were talking to locals and just having fun. In typical GI fashion however, one of our group got a little too intoxicated. He was a short, stocky rough and tumble type of guy that became somewhat unruly when he drank. You know how it is, some guys become lovers when plied with alcohol, others have to try and prove something, anyway it seems that the mixture of youth, testosterone and alcohol just doesn't't blend that well.

"Back off……..Back off or I'll kill you" breaks the monotone level of speech in the bar.

"Yea boy, you just go ahead and try it," is the retort.

Nino, and Sal were at the shuffle board table as I stood close by, learning the object of the game.

The two men were now standing, facing off, and from what I could see, it was a local cowboy, and Charlie Swenson, ready to do battle.

Charlie, while one of us, stood holding an empty quart bottle that he had grabbed from behind the bar, and was getting ready to hit this guy over the head with the bottle.

All activities within the saloon became overshadowed, as everyone focused on the two engaged in this heated argument.

Some one from our group quickly intervened by grabbing the empty bottle from Charlie's hand, while another of the group tried to reason with him. This was to no avail, and the situation began to get out of control, as the inebriated soldiers logic was so distorted. He wanted to fight, and threatened to take on the whole bar.

Out of the blue someone spins around the drunken serviceman and cold-cocks him, launching him from his position standing by the bar, sliding down the sawdust covered floor. He must have slid ten feet from the impact of that shot, as he wobbly tried to get to his feet.

"Boy, you better save some of that fight for them Japs" he blurted out in a Texas accent, as he turned and went back to his seat.

The punch had done what words were incapable of doing. It was not intended to knock him out, but just bring him back to reality. I recall it was Billy, the left gunner that threw that intervening punch, and I guess it was the right thing to do, as everything immediately quieted down. The would-be trouble maker was down, sitting at a table, his head resting on the tabletop, sleeping off the stupor.

"I just hate people who can't handle their liquor," said Billy

"This idiot's gonna give me a bad name in my home state of Texas" he spewed. "Can't let that happen."

Now there were at least 10 of us GI's in the bar at the time and in hind sight I can't really blame the proprietor for calling the authorities.

I'm sure he thought that the situation was getting out of hand, and before the situation came to total lawlessness there had to be some intervention. Although we had succeeded in defusing the situation among ourselves, the damage had already been done.

We all had moved from the shuffle-board table, back to the bar, and were enjoying a beer, when the door opens and a Texas lawman swaggers into the bar, probably within five minutes of the incident.

While everyone had turned to see who had come in, the sheriff's presence caused no alarming reaction to anyone in our group. He was of average height, sort of stocky built, but wore thick Coke bottle eyeglasses.

"Look who just walked in, I think it's Wyatt Earp" comment one of the more playful, and less tactful members of our group. Then, in his semi-inebriated state, does a double take look at the sheriff, and commented on his thick glasses.

"I don't think this bastard can see shit," he said as we all begin to howl with laughter. Overhearing the comment, the peace officer looked around for the evidence of smirks on our faces, and headed towards us. Not a smart thing for us to do under the circumstances, and he did not take kindly to that comment, so from that point on unknowingly, we were in deep trouble. He just nodded his head, pausing and eyeing each of us as he slowly passed by. He was remembering our faces.

In a typical Texas accent he demanded to know what had happened. The bartender spoke to him privately at the other end of the bar. After a brief exchange of words the sheriff then approached the GI that had caused the problem, waking him from his stupor by prodding him back to consciousness.

He began questioning him as he woke, and the soldier seemed incoherent in his responses. The officer was intolerant of the drunk, and his nodding off while being questioned. He continued prodding him, until the drunken soldier stood up and was getting ready to take a swing at the sheriff.

"Just let him sleep it off" Sal yelled from the other side of the bar.

"We'll take care of him" came a voice from the same direction.

Now being the least intoxicated of everyone there, I spoke up and told the officer that everything was under control now and I explained what had happened.

"Look, things got a little out of hand, but we've got it under control" I said

"He was just blowing off some steam, everything's all right now."

Now that might have flown had there not been that idiotic comment when he walked in. Someone was going to pay for that disrespectful episode and being that I was doing the talking, I guess I was elected.

"Boy, you better sit down and watch your mouth b-fore I take you in for interuptin my investigation" the lawman blurted out.

He now turned and approached me, and in a brutalizing manner and tone he unleashed his wrath towards me.

"Look, there was no harm done here," and I again apologized for the actions and said that we would all leave soon. His approach toward me had ended just inches from my nose, and he stood so uncomfortably close to me that I could smell the stench of his breath. As he began provoking me, I stepped backwards away from the vile odor of his mouth. I made a face reflecting the offensive nature of his breath, while fanning the noxious odor from my face. The crew members began howling with laughter in their drunken state as they thought this was comedic. That was the second foolish thing I had done. Even the locals chuckled to the dismay of the officer. I was sober and matching wits with this guy because I hadn't done anything wrong. Realizing I might have belittled his authority I said,

"Look, I'm sorry, we were all just kidding around and we'll be leaving very soon" and I turned toward the stool, rejoining my friends. At this point the sheriff positioned himself in front of me blocking my path. I paused, looked him square in the eye and said, in what I thought to be a respectful manner,

32

"What are you talking about, you've got no real jurisdiction over us anyway."

That was the third idiotic thing that was done. Instead of defusing the situation, I had made it worse.

Nino and Salvatore had jumped up, and were coming to my aid when the officer reached for his weapon.

"Sit down you two, just back off" said the sheriff, stopping both in their tracks.

The next thing I knew I was hand cuffed, and was being hauled off with the drunken GI to the local jail.

We were forced to spend the night behind bars, and believe me it was no fun. I didn't really even know this drunken jerk that I had gone to bat for, and because of him, I was locked up. What made matters even worse, was that I was placed in a cell with the idiot. It was a long sleepless night.

Looking back on it now, I guess that sheriff had to do something, especially in front of the locals to save face and defend his authority. I should have been smart enough to get the whole crew out of there right after the incident, but hind sight is always 20/20. I must have seemed like a wise guy to that small town sheriff, and maybe I had undermined him, but I hadn't done anything wrong. Kind of makes you think twice about speaking up.

Anyway, the next morning the MP's were summoned to the jail house and proceeded to take us back to the base. That entire trip back to the base was filled with guilt on my part. I had never been in trouble with the law, and was embarrassed of what repercussions might follow.

Once back at the base, we immediately received notice that our Commanding Officer wanted to see us at his headquarters, on the double. So we were escorted to him.

The now sober GI told his story to the Commander, stating that he had been egged on and provoked. Looking as bad as he must have felt the C/O reprimanded him and stated that another incident such as this one would have him brought up on charges. I guess that this wasn't the first time that an incident of this type had happened to him, as the Commander had a file on him.

He then turned to me and motioned for my explanations. I began to explain the story, what I had done to avert the problem. I explained that I had been duped and made the scapegoat for trying to intervene. I apologized and also promised that I would never do such a foolish thing again. I had learned the hard way to keep my mouth shut.

We were both dismissed and left the office. I kept my distance from that guy, as I thought he was nothing but trouble, and soon rejoined my group and the activities of the day.

The guys were so happy to see me, and thought it was great the way I stood up to the sheriff. They laughed at the fun things that had happened, and were sorry that I had to spend the night in jail.

"Hey Nick, we tried to grab a rope, and a jeep, and we were gonna bust-a you out of that jailhouse" said Nino, "but everyone got a-so lit-up that we couldn't remember where they took a-you." We all laughed again and welcomed each other back. What a great bunch of guys.

It was more than a month since the bar incident, and the next seven day pass would be our last in Clovis, New Mexico. I knew our training was over, and of our plans to be shipped overseas, so I took the opportunity to go home to see my family. This would be the last time I would have to visit them before facing the enemy, and felt obligated to do so. From Clovis I boarded a train to Chicago, then to Penn Station, New York. I then hopped another train to Penn Station, Newark. After that it was a short bus trip to Paterson which equated to a full 2 days of travel.

It was sure great to be home and see my family again. All the relatives came over to see me, and I looked for some of my old friends, although most had been drafted.

"You're so thin do they feed you enough over there" my parents commented.

"I'm fine" I replied, "but where's Pete," I hadn't seen him and I missed my younger brother.

"He enlisted in the Navy" my sister replied, as a whimper came from my mother.

"It's OK mom, he'll be fine" I said reassuringly.

Frankly, I was amazed to hear of his enlistment. I still thought of him as just a little kid, and now he too was serving his country, where had the time gone.

It was still wonderful to spend time with my parents, to see them happy, and proud of me. By this time I had gotten my Sergeant stripes, and on Sunday I went to church and prayed for a safe return home. I saw many friends, and people I had known my entire life, and was acknowledged during the sermon.

. I also saw the girl that I really liked in church, while at that time she wasn't really my girlfriend, although we were writing each other often. This was the woman that was to become my future wife, and I was so glad to see her, and I went over to talk to her. We began with an embrace, and set out to make some plans for a date, when I was interrupted by my sister and her girlfriends. I confirmed the date, with Dot for later that week, and was Shanghaied into introductions and spending time talking to my sisters friends.

Dot and I had a wonderful time together, as we saw a show and grabbed an ice cream cone together while we walked and talked about things, and I felt very comfortable with her. I told her that I would write to her while overseas, and she said she would continue writing, and then she told me to be careful, and to come home safe.

The next day I went to Newark to see my future brother-in-law, Steve Kalivas, who was working as a manager of the Union News Bar, in Newark's Penn Station. He was a nice guy and we had always gotten along well. We talked for a while, as I nursed a Beer at the bar, as he continued about his business as manager. He disappeared for a while and returned with five quarts of liquor as a gift for me to take back with me. He knew I didn't drink and I thought it was a strange gift. His thoughts however were from the heart as he said,

"I'm sure you'll find some good use for it." I guess this was his way of bringing some happiness to the GI's. So, as not to appear ungrateful, I carried the booty back home with me, which was no easy task. I made it back home lugging this cache.

With the week pass nearly over and having spent much of the time traveling just to get to my destination, I said my goodbyes to my family and friends, and started my long trip back to New Mexico. I boarded at Penn Station Newark, and connected to Penn NY and as usual the train was jammed packed with people and GI's. It was so crowded, I didn't even have a seat so I stayed in the vestibule sitting on the half case of liquor I was carrying. I guess it got a little better the further west we got, and I even managed a few hours of sleep while still sitting in the vestibule on my way to Chicago. After switching trains there and procuring a comfortable seat, I estimated that I was only half way to New Mexico, so I tried to sleep as much as possible while traveling across America. While considerably more tolerable then the first leg of the journey it was still not great and after what seemed like an eternity, I finally arrived back in Clovis. The trip was long but well worth it, and I felt good after having seen my family.

Chapter VI

Chapter VI

Going Overseas

Within days of my return, our training at Clovis was over, and our orders from headquarters read that crew number 70 (our crew) was to be sent over seas to replace a crew that was shot down on a mission over Formosa (Taiwan). We would be part of the 58th Bomb Wing of the 20Th Air Force. This was a newly formed Wing of the Air Force and we had no idea what role or significance we would play in it. Obviously we were being trained to attack Japan and it would not be for some time that we became aware of the fact that the 58th Bomb Wing of the 20th Air Force was comprised of the cream of the crop of all the men of basic training. We were being rated on all our abilities throughout our training and had been deemed to be the top. As a result of this, we had the privilege and distinction of being part of "The 58th".

On November 7th, 1944 we flew on a C-54 from Clovis to LaGuardia airport in New York. We were transported to an Army processing area where we got our various shots and were prepared to travel overseas. We were all put up at a hotel close to the airfield.

Nino says to me, "Come on, let's grab a cab, and hop into Manhattan."

I was game, and we left our hotel looking for some excitement.

"Where's Sal, lets grab him too" I suggested.

"A-where do you think Sal is, he was hungry and went to look for something to eat, as usual" Nino replied.

We started our evening at the world famous Stork Club where the Big Bands were playing, and we blended in with the crowd, dancing and romancing.

At that time there were many men in uniform, mostly officers, but we were having a great time dancing up a storm. Not many enlisted men knew the hot spots of NYC, so we were rubbing elbows with the elite, and doing fine.

We told the ladies that we met that we were off to fight the war in Japan tomorrow, and needles to say, a man in uniform, going off to fight for his country in the morning, we were very popular.

That evening, I recall seeing a few women dressed in full length fur coats, high heels, with nothing else on underneath. They flashed their wares at us, obviously of the professional persuasion if you catch my drift. I guess they were there to meet the special needs of young men going off to war.

Nino, the consummate gentleman that he was, inebriated or not, tipped his hat to the trollops and proceeded to thank them.

"Dearest ladies, I wanna thank-a you for doing a-your part for the war effort, for without you, and Amore"..........

"Nino, let's get out of here'" I said, interrupting his pseudo eloquence, as I hailed a cab back to the hotel, and we were off.

Bright and early on the 9th we boarded a plane and headed for Bermuda, the first leg of our journey. We were given food and lodging that evening, and continued on the next morning to the Azores in the Atlantic Ocean. From that point we went to Casablanca, Tripoli Tania in North Africa and then to Cairo, Egypt. We were given sleeping accommodations in barracks as well as food at the mess halls in all the air bases we stopped at.

In Cairo I remember seeing an MP reprimanding an Egyptian civilian who had worked on the base in the mess hall. The worker had two loaves of round bread stashed under his hat. It was so obvious to the MP and to anyone else looking at the guy that he had something on top of his head. The MP tried to explain to him that he could eat on the base but that it was against orders for anyone to take food off the base. Naturally the MP confiscated the two loaves of bread. I could understand why the Egyptian had taken the bread after seeing the poverty and despair of the people in Cairo. Most people that we saw there were gaunt; mostly unshaven wearing basically rags of tattered unmatched clothing. Those that were fortunate enough to have shoes were usually worn beyond their usefulness. It seemed that these people lacked even the basic necessities for survival.

Our trip continued, each day landing in a new location, spending the night and leaving the next morning. We left Cairo and went to Abad an, Iran. We then went on to three locations in India: Karachi, Agra and the last being Kharagpur Air Base. This was one of four bases of the 20th Bomber Command that were located in India built specifically to accommodate the B-29.

I had to say goodbye to my buddies Sal, and Nino for a while, as they were stationed in another place in India, and those guys were greatly missed by me.

Chapter VII

Kharagpur, India

This was to be our new home, the 468th Bomb Group and Kharagpur was the command headquarters of all bases in India. Of the other three bases, Chakulia housed the 40th Dunhkundi, was home to the 444th and Piardoba served the 796th group. We were all part of the newly formed 58th Bomb Wing of the 20th Air Force, established with the sole purpose of taking the war to the Japanese mainland. After that eight-day trip and having traveled half way around the world, we were given a day or so to get oriented to our new surroundings and the operations we would undertake.

The heat was almost unbearable as soon as we got out of the plane. There was a hot wind which blew this red hued dust around in circular mini-tornados. Just breathing made your lungs feel seared. We had stayed in barracks at every stop through out our trip but this place was by far the worst.

"What the hell are we doing in this God forsaken place?" I thought to myself. While no one had expected Miami Beach, this place was out and out primitive. There was no sense in complaining but as we were given a tour of the base, the conditions were addressed and acknowledged by our superior officers. They knew the living accommodations were a tad Spartan as they put it, but we had a job to do and we were to make the best of it.

Our barracks were constructed of concrete with walls approximately 7 feet high, topped by a thatched roof, supported by three inch tree trunks running the entire 60 foot length. These roofs were made of a sort of reeds that were woven together in a primitive manner. They reminded me of grass shacks, something that Robinson Crusoe would have built. I vividly remembered reading that story and the problems of rats and other vermin that had plagued him. I recalled the details of these creatures nibbling at his toes as he tried to sleep. Needless to say, we too had the same misfortune, an infestation of something stirring above us. That first night I did not sleep well because of the rustling of vermin on the roof. I kept my feet covered and even thought of sleeping with my boots on. We complained in the morning and the problem was rectified that day as the rustling on the roof stopped. There were however these lizards that were all around. On occasion a large snake would find its way into the barracks making life interesting to say the least.

At 20 feet wide, these units housed seven man groups of six crews of enlisted men for a total of 42 men. Our beds were constructed of primitive cut lumber with rope lashed to the frame to support a mattress. Above us was a canopy that housed mosquito netting, a necessity for disease control while sleeping in this part of the world. With 42 men living together, to help keep some order, we had a local man and two helpers that worked with us to keep the barracks in good shape. Their job was to clean the barracks and to keep everything in order. They also cared for the laundering and pressing of our uniforms and other clothing. The oldest was about thirty years old; I think his name was Jaipuria. The two helpers were in their late teens. For these conveniences every GI in the barracks paid the sum of one rupee per week. At that time a rupee equated to twenty three cents in American currency. Jaipuria received a grand total of $9.66 American and gave each of his helper's one rupee each (23 cents). These young guys did the majority of the work but Jaipuria was a true entrepreneur and these men were elated to work for him and us. We learned later on that this was the most money that they had ever made in their lives. So we slowly settled into our new home and tried to become more at ease with the conditions in India. We learned of the differences and similarities of our cultures.

India Barracks and Orderlies

Our grounds school training continued and we began training missions of bombing practice within days of our arrival. Second Lt. William Wills piloted the plane as we began trying our bombing skills on a sandbar. These were dummy bombs just designed to simulate a bombing run. This was an exercise in coordination with emphasis on handling primarily for pilot and bombardier. This by no means left the rest of the crew with nothing to do. We all had our jobs to do during every facet of operations. There was a certain protocol of procedure and check lists that were to be strictly observed without deviation. These were to take place before, during and after each flight. These included both visual and physical inspections by the crew. This encompassed every crew member and aided in our safety so they were taken very seriously. We all had an area that was close enough to our stations that we could do a visual inspection. We then had to report back to the pilot, being that he was in control. The pilot was responsible for the safety of both crew and plane. In the event of any mishaps, the pilot would be held accountable and would bear the brunt of any mishaps. We had all memorized our checklists and while still somewhat tense from our lack of experience, we managed to complete our first practice run. The area that these exercises of gunnery and bombing practice took place was on a small uninhabited island called Halliday Island, located in the Bay of Bengal, India.

With that completed our next objective was for the pilot to learn to maneuver the plane with a full bomb load that weighed in at 139,000 pounds, thus allowing both crew and pilot an opportunity to better get the feel of the aircraft. Just to put that into perspective, this plane was close to 70 tons when loaded, and aside from the puzzling fact of how it was possible to get off the ground, there was special emphasis on the bombardier in regulating the release and distribution of bombs from each bomb bay for balance and weight distribution. We spent weeks on these training bombing runs gaining experience and know-how on the inner mechanics of the bomber, and became cohesive a unit.

On a trip to a nearby town one of the crew members stationed in our barracks saw a merchant with a small monkey that had been trained to sit on his shoulder. Being far from home and thinking this would be a great pet, the GI offered to purchase it. After much haggling they both agreed on a price. The GI brought this newly acquired treasure back to base to live with us in the barracks. This was a wild monkey and while it was kind of cute, most of us were afraid of it. Who knew what kind of disease that this thing might have.

Most of us were opposed to the monkey staying in the barracks. The GI pleaded with us insisting that the monkey would be no trouble at all. He claimed it would be tethered at night and wouldn't disrupt anything. We reluctantly agreed.

All went well for the majority of the early evening as we continued our duties. By the time we were in bed all seemed fine. The monkey had settled down, and everyone was down for the evening. We had been sleeping for a few hours when suddenly, a major commotion began within the barracks. There began this high pitched, deafening screech accompanied by a blood curdling scream. Most of us woke frantically thinking we were under attack as this whirlwind made its way through the barracks.

"What in the hell is going on" I said to my friend Shep.

"I don't know, maybe it's an air raid" he replied

"It's in the barracks" I said as I grabbed my 45, pulled the pistol from the shoulder holster "maybe it's a tiger or something."

There was this horrendous noise at deafening decibels as this intruder began jumping demonically throughout the barracks, while startling the hell out of us. From cot to cot he jumped, climbing the mosquito netting. He then started swinging from the rafters of the roof while emitting more of these deafening shrill screams. To my disbelief there were still a few crew members still asleep. To those that had the misfortune of being awakened by this deranged monkey jumping on them thought they were being attacked by a Hyena or wild dog.

Within a minute, everyone in the barracks was up and trying to catch the insane little demon as he jumped to an fro leaving behind him a trail of disarray in the once organized bunk house. Luckily this little urchin made its escape thru an open window, his owner in hot pursuit, departing before facing the wrath of the rest of us. After two hours got the monkey was calm enough to be held, and the owner wisely spent the remainder of the evening elsewhere, comforting his rescued pet. Apparently the monkey had chewed through its leash during the evening. He had become frightened by its new environment and made an attempt to depart.

We all tried as best we could to get back to sleep but we were all so pumped full of adrenalin from the escapade that most found it difficult, however I wasn't one of those unfortunates, and fell back to sleep among the disarray of our barracks.

We arose the following morning and assessed the condition of our home. We straightened things out while we set some new rules for our little guest. They weren't too strict, but fair enough that we would be insured of our sleep in the evenings. The rules were that the monkey was to be caged and left outside. That was far enough so as not to be heard throughout the evenings. The pet's owner was more than happy to oblige our wishes and all went well with the new arrangements. Within a few days the monkey had become much better behaved and we all started to become more at ease with its presence. His stay with us however was brief. It only lasted a few weeks as the crew member that owned the monkey vanished after our second mission. The reason for his disappearance was never brought to our attention. No one knew whether he quit flying because of the anticipated pressure of combat or something else. One day he was just gone along with all of his belongings including the monkey.

On one of our early training missions we were using a type of live bombs and ammunitions. These bombs had safety devices that were to be removed while in flight, thus arming them prior to being dropped from the plane. It was my job, as the right blister gunner to remove these pins and get the bombs activated for detonation on the target.

"Bombardier to right gunner..... over" came the message from the intercom

"This is the right gunner" I responded

"Nick, we'll be over the target area in about 15 minutes, get started in activating the bombs... over" ordered the bombardier.

"Roger" I responded

I entered the bomb bays and began removing the safety's that I could reach, walking along the 12 inch catwalk that ran the entire length of the bomb bays. Hindered by the bulkiness of my full back parachute and without giving it a second thought, I took it off and continued the task of removing the pins. At a certain level, I was unable to reach the other bombs that extended an additional four feet blow the catwalk, so I hoped right on the bomb bay doors and continued my business. I was standing on these doors walking around on them, and upon completion, reentered the bulk headed area of the rear compartment carrying my parachute.

"What are you doing" said Tex as he looked at me in astonishment, his eyes the size of silver dollars.

"Where's your chute" asked Shep, "why did you take it off?"

"It was so bulky back there and there wasn't enough room to reach the pins, so I took it off" I replied. "The bomb bay doors were closed, everything's alright."

"Alright, are you crazy, don't you remember that these hydraulic bomb bay doors are designed to release automatically, you know, the safety feature, when 125 lbs of pressure is placed on them. Don't you remember that" said Shep.

I weighed 118 pounds at that time and I was thankful of that. We had supposedly learned about this in ground school, I guess I was playing hooky that day. God certainly was with me that day, as even today, I still get chills as I think what might have happened to me. I could have dropped 4000 feet, without a parachute, sitting atop an activated bomb, riding it to my death! I guess it was my enthusiasm that made me not think of the consequences of my actions. I never made that mistake again; thank God.

Another lesson was learned in the early stages of my stay at Kharagpur, as I went to take a shower mid-afternoon. It was dreadfully hot, and I thought a shower would cool me off. I hadn't realized that the pipes from the water tower to the showers were above ground baking in the sun, and as the water hit me I was almost scalded by the intense heat. These were not pressurized hot and cold running water showers. Instead, they were just large tanks that used thermal energy to heat the water. There was no regulating the temperature in the shower because there was no cold water. As a result, the water from the storage tank would become so hot that it could blister your skin. That was the first and last time I showered in the afternoon. I learned to shower in the early mornings or evenings as our scheduled missions dictated.

The heat's intensity in the afternoons caused our planes to become so hot that we were not allowed near them. The inside temperature would exceed 200 degrees, so as a result all mission flights were either in the morning or early evening. With daily mid-day temperatures that high, nothing could be done in such oppressive heat. The afternoons were spent resting or taking 'siestas' to escape this treacherous heat. It was at least 100 degrees most days in India, and could exceed 140 on occasion. It was an oppressive heat, not being completely unbearable for a 22 year old, but let's face it, 100 degrees is still tough to handle. The air force gave us a canned grapefruit juice, everyday in an effort to thin our blood. I don't know if that actually did anything or not for us but we were told to drink it.

This extreme heat not only took its toll on us but also wreaked havoc with the mechanical components of our planes. There were constant problems with the over heating; this lead to frequent emergency fires. It seemed that the cooling system of cowlings designed to let air into the rear cylinders of the rotary engine had proved to be inadequate. As a result, the engines were prone to severe overheating problems. Compounding the seriousness of the problem was a hidden problem within the engines that proved to be the cause of these inextinguishable fires.

Magnesium was used in many of the inner engine components. Magnesium is a wonderful metal whose physical weight is one third that of steel and had much greater strength than aluminum. Its use was implemented within the aircraft in an effort to save weight. While the engineers were successful in their quest in weight reduction, they created a much larger problem. It turns out that magnesium is subject to cracking under stress and heat. It's also extremely flammable, and making matters even worse, when magnesium ignites, it burns at a much higher temperature than the surrounding metal. It burns with such ferocity that it is almost impossible to extinguish. What this meant to crews of the B-29 is there was a constant threat of engine fire that had the potential to engulf and melt the entire wing completely off the plane. There was just a 90-second time frame in the event of a major engine fire, before the bulkheads of the firewall would be compromised and our wings would be susceptible. There were extinguishers in the engine compartment that were employed when a fire began however if the fire wasn't extinguished quickly, it meant serious trouble. With tremendously large fuel tanks located in the wings behind the engines if the fire penetrated the firewall the plane would explode when the fuel tanks ignited.

This bomber had gone from design to production without the usual rigorous testing procedures that planes are subject to. The urgency of the war and the need to produce a long range bomber resulted in sidestepping the usual protocol testing. There were many glitches in the planes. As a result, alterations that would normally have been done pre-production were now being done in the field.

Engineers from Boeing were flown into India to make alterations to the cowlings in an effort to bring additional cooling air into these engines. All their mechanical efforts were futile. Ultimately, a larger engine, supplied by Pratt & Whitney replaced the Wright Cyclones. The Wasp, as it was called, was more powerful than its predecessor, developing 3500 HP and ran considerably cooler. Changes that would have taken considerable time to repair resulting from design flaws were now being addressed mostly in the trenches.

Retooling of the machinery at the factory would have wasted a considerable amount of time, as the shops would have to stop production while the new equipment was installed or the machines re-tooled. As a result, refinements to the plane were gradually implemented throughout the evolution of the B-29. The results were evident as all mechanical problems that had enveloped the early production planes subsided thru its development.

While considerable progress was made in rectifying design and engineering flaws, flight in the B-29 was never without risk. There were three portions during every mission that bombers are under the most stress that increased the vulnerability and therefore susceptibility for disaster to occur. These are by no means listed in any order of importance, but just written as a partial list of potential dangers we faced on an almost daily basis. There were a host of other variables that could contribute to disaster, but the obvious ones were, during takeoffs, followed by the assault over the target, and finally landing safely on the ground.

Take-offs, were always cause for concern and the problematic engines and extreme heat further complicated it. Our aircraft weighted in at 139,000 pounds and coaxing a craft of this size and weight into flight is not an easy task even under the most optimum conditions.

The weather conditions in India contribute to a constant stillness and heaviness in the air due to the extreme heat and humidity. As a result our bloated aircraft constantly struggled to attain the lift needed to become airborne. These conditions and extreme heat create a phenomenon that decreases the air density, and all but eliminating the lift. This lack of density is problematic, and as a result, the controls of the plane are not nearly as responsive, thus forcing the engines to struggle to power the plane into flight. On most takeoffs, upon getting off the ground, it seems as though we hugged the earth at an altitude of 500 feet for miles, then we would gradually ascend to the altitude for a safe flight. This is not a comforting thought, nor is it a healthy situation when you have a full bomb load and are loaded to capacity with aviation fuel.

Following takeoff, the next most dangerous time in a bomber was while flying over the target. The pilot relinquishes control of the craft to the bombardier, who has calculated the exact point and time to release the bomb load. During that time prior to bombs away, there is no evasive actions that can be taken to avoid enemy flak, so our only defenses were from our own resolve against whatever enemy fighters were sent up to destroy us. This defense of the plane was my area of expertise.

Finally, after completing the all of the above there was of course, landing the plane after a mission. This was again a dangerous task, be it for maneuvering with damage sustained during combat, running low on fuel or any of a host of other variables that could go wrong, but during these three separate instances of a mission was when most planes were lost.

As we began to tolerate this hell-hole that we were forced to live in, as there was no getting use to it, the first holiday we celebrated was Thanksgiving. So to keep morale up, our supply ships brought in canned turkey and some of the usual Thanksgiving fare to help us celebrate. The food here was never that good to begin with, there was just something about the constant heat, and the likes of powdered eggs and the usual breakfast fare that made them particularly unpalatable to me. There was a constant threat of dysentery, diarrhea whether from the excessive heat, or the fact that everything spoiled so quickly that left us all with constant stomach problems. However, the government tried to rectify these problems, but conditions were slow to change.

Knowing full well that holidays were always the roughest times for the troops, the government would always do a little extra for us on these lonely times away from home. Whether thru entertainment, special passes, or traditional holiday foods, something was always done to keep up morale.

Being Thanksgiving, our menu consisted of turkey, spaghetti, vegetables and assorted cakes for dessert. While no substitute for being home, the drab mess hall was embellished with decorations and white tablecloths adorned the cafeteria style tables for the occasion, and in seeing this, my thoughts momentarily drifted away from India and the unpleasantness of war.

I became happy, at least for a while, and stood in line and chose the foods that I liked best for this holiday feast. It looked and smelled like real food and as I got my food and sat down to begin eating, I noticed something odd in my plate. I saw some black specks in my food that looked like extremely large pieces of black pepper. Upon closer examination I saw what appeared to be legs on them. Turning to the other crew members I said,

"Hey French, do you see some spots in this chow."

"I hadn't noticed any till now," replied French

"Man I see them; I hope they're not moving Shep chimed in.

We all came to the same conclusion, that they were in fact bugs. I was kind of a finicky eater anyway, but this totally ruined my appetite. I went to the captain of the mess hall, tray in hand and complained that my dinner had bugs in it. He closely examined the meal and tried to downplay what he saw.

44

"I think its just spices" he said in an effort to appease me. Respectfully, I answered,

"Sir, I don't know what kind of spices the Army cooks with, but the ones that I'm used to don't have legs." I looked at him square in the eye, and he replied sheepishly,

"Don't worry, eat your dinner, even if it is bugs they won't hurt you. You'll be getting more protein." He suggested that I get something else, but by that time the holiday spirit had all but vanished, along with my appetite. I sat down again, pushed the plate away, and focused on my dessert of pumpkin pie. But after some serious visual scrutiny, although it didn't look bad, I just no longer had an appetite so I left the mess hall.

What started out to be a special day, and with all the decorations was very nice, and it did make us momentarily forget the unpleasantness of where we were. But the conditions under which we lived were not healthy, and most of us found that by not eating much, our stomach problems lessened.

In early December, the Air Force gave us a seven day pass, so some of us decided it would be exciting to visit Calcutta, so we all boarded a train from our base to the famous city. The train was not the type of train that we are used to traveling on in America. The train used wood or coal for fuel and stopped continuously for water to make steam. The rail cars were made of wood, not the iron or aluminum that we were used to in America. They were rickety and had very small compartments to sit in. They reminded me of the trains I had seen in history books in school as a kid, looked to be modeled after a French design.

After three uncomfortable hours of travel sharing the crowded train and making numerous stops for water, we finally arrived in Calcutta. What I saw there has remained with me my entire life.

India had been called The Land of Enchantment, and Calcutta was a major city. The people of India are of two classes, the rich and the extremely poor. With their caste system, the poor greatly outnumber the rich. From the train station we were inundated with the sights of such misery, the likes of which I had never experienced before.

I saw beggars everywhere, people dressed in what appeared to be rags throughout the station almost to the point that I thought we were mistakenly dropped off in a leper colony. There were disfigurements and deformities of sickening proportions as we made our way from the train station. These poor miserable souls were begging for pennies, and apparently were living on the streets. I witnessed such deplorable conditions and the suffering of these people that I reached in my pocket to give something to them. I then witnessed a person drinking water from the gutter that seemed to have sewage in it, just sickening to think of what terrible lives these people had.

"Oh my god, let's get out of here" I said to Shep

"Which way do we go" he replied

"Beats me, let's just follow the crowd, this place gives me the willies" as I motioned to follow the crowd scurrying from the station.

"Boy I hope these beggars are confined to the area close to the train station," said Shep.

"Well, it makes sense that they would congregate at the train station, where the visual impact would be the greatest. I don't see how any non suspecting visitors would not take pity on these poor souls, but I wish someone at the base would have warned us on what to expect here" I commented.

Shep just looked at me nodding his head in agreement.

As we exited from the train station, I again witnessed sights that I had never experienced. While the beggars had lessened there were crowds of people everywhere, and animals all over the streets. It seemed as though there was no order, almost chaotic. There were cars and taxies that were stuck in this amalgam of beasts, humans, and machine, and progress was made at a snails pace. Horns blew incessantly from the motorized vehicles, but their progress was hindered by the oxen and chickens and the sheer confusion in the streets. I saw a few non conventional taxies that were burning wood in their trunks; I guess they had been converted to run on steam, which added to the heat and smoke to an already sweltering place.

Our progress had not amounted to a block from the train station in the half hour we had proceeded, and while conditions seemed slightly better than in the train station there were still sights that shocked me. People living on the streets in extreme poverty, was not the half of it. I noticed what appeared to be an elderly person lying dead in the street, as vultures attacked the carcass. Most seemed unfazed by the filth and death surrounding them, while others walked aimlessly through the city. This certainly did not seem like a Land of Enchantment to me. This initial experience took me by complete shock and surprise.

I saw some rickshaws that were pulled by some natives, and they seemed to maneuver their way around the streets better than taxis, so we hailed one to take us to our hotel. Soon the poverty was not my primary focal point, as we maneuvered away from the main overcrowded streets to our hotel.

"Thank god we're out of that mess" I said to Shep

"You're not kidding, I tell you I almost got back on the train when I saw how things were here," Shep replied.

"I never expect it to be Coney Island here, but we're here, so lets have a look around and , if it's not to our liking we'll get the hell out of here tomorrow" I said.

We checked in to an open air hotel that was clean, settled in and then proceeded to sightsee, and there were so many things to see everywhere.

From snake charmers to ancient temples we were never without something to see or do. One thing that I recall was that the buildings appeared to sweat, like a glass of cold water being out in the sweltering sun. I'm sure it was due to the heat but again, a strange phenomenon to see.

The rickshaws for hire seemed to be the best means of transportation within the city. The drivers knew the streets, and communications seemed not to be a problem, although the accents were strange to us. Two of us would board as the hack would take us to our destination. For that, these people would charge three pyce, the equivalent of three cents American. They were outside of our hotel and always seemed attuned to recommend guiding us to Chowringe Road the area of commerce within the city. With many shops located on the main road that catered to the upper end souvenirs that most wealthy tourist would be interested in. Carved Ivory seemed to be the most desirable commodity offered, as were silver bracelets and other handmade jewelry.

This area was devoid of the squalor we had seen previously, and seemed a different world from the poverty and despair we had witnessed upon our arrival.

In one store I happen to notice a small sledge hammer, maybe 8 pounds or so, and as I lifted it up to question the price, Shep asked me "what the hell do you want that for."

"Insurance" I replied, as the clerk informed of the reasonably priced item. "Two pyce is not a bad price to pay for some insurance, is it?" I questioned Shep.

Bewildered, he shrugged his shoulders as we walked out with the hammer

A right or left turn off Chowringe Road brought you back to the reality of life in Calcutta. Local red light districts of the town abounded, and these bordellos catered to whatever degenerate activities you could imagine and then some. Between the drivers suggesting, or recommending a good place rather coyly in that distinct accent as they would wink, wink and nod, nod and smile. They must have gotten some sort of a commission for everyone they procured, there were also little kids that would come up to you and asking, Jig, Jig sahib sort of in a melodious tone.

"Jig-Jig sahib….. does this kid want to do a dance for us" Shep asked.

"Beats the hell out of me, but I don't think that this kid knows the Irish Jig," I replied as we both chuckled. This kid must have been 10 years old, and at first I thought he was begging. "Here you go sonny" as Shep handed him some change.

"No..Jig-Jig Sahib, No Jig-Jig ???" as the youngster looks puzzled but stashes the loot.

The driver motions for the kid to leave, saying something inaudible to us, but sounding irritated, he again, in a louder more assertive tone forces the youngster away from us rather abruptly. The driver then explained that "Jig-Jig" was a slang word for a sexual act, and that this little bastard was procuring clients, or rather Johns for his sister that worked in the world's oldest profession. Furthermore his sister was12 years old, and was sick as he put it, probable suffering from some type of V.D.

"His 12 year old sister, no way" Shep responds,

"What kind of degenerate would sell his sister, and what kind of animal would want to do that to a 12 year old kid" I said in disgust.

"You want, I take you to a good place, sahib, clean woman, very pretty woman-very pretty" the driver suggests.

"No thanks, we're OK," we replied.

"Hey the driver was pissed off at the kid, I guess he was worried that the kid was cutting in on his action" Shep said in a low voice.

"I guess, but that young Jig-Jiger was eyeing you up to become his brother-in-law" I said to Shep laughingly.

"No way" answered Shep "didn't you notice he was a little cock-eyed, and was talking to you"" as we both started laughing.

"I don't understand the Jig-Jig part of the equation" I said to Shep

"Beats me" he replies.

"Must be the squeaking of the box spring when you're taking care of business" I said, as we both laughed.

We were warned during our initial orientation upon arrival to India that there was an epidemic of venereal disease. Supposedly, 98 % of the population suffered from the ailment, and I guess they meant the Professional Population so as a result; many were reluctant to pursue that type of entertainment. Others had no problem with relieving stress, and felt that they were adequately protected by the normal means of contraception of the day. However after hearing of the rate of infection, it kind of takes the wind out of your sails, and I wouldn't't feel safe in that situation unless I was wearing a wet suit.

There was so much to see and such a different culture that something new would amaze me on a daily basis.

I had never before neither seen nor even heard of cremation before visiting India. This was the normal procedure for disposing of the dead, being sanctified by their religion. However for an outsider it was somewhat strange to experience. Depending on the wealth of the deceased, a bier of wood, eight feet tall would be stacked. Your wealth would determine whether the stacked wood would be fast or slow burning. The body would be placed atop this bier as the family paid last respects, then when all was done they ignited the mound. This was not a private ceremony here in India, but done in the open with many people in attendance watching. While either mourners, acquaintances of the family or other, this seemingly was a type of social event in this culture, and there was a crowd gathering.

I had no desire to watch this happen and I turned my head and began walking away as the bier was lit. I was startled by hysterical screams and gasps, and as I turned towards the commotion. I witnessed what appeared to be people running towards, and then surrounding the open blaze. From what I could gather in all the confusion, the deceased's wife had jumped into the flames to die with her husband, not wanting to face the hardships of life without him. I thank God I didn't see it, but even the thought of that was horrific.

While somewhat alien to the culture, I found my stay in India to be a mostly pleasant experience of an exotic land and culture. The food was not my favorite, although I am sure we were tainted because of the constant stomach problems even back at the base.

The off-time was wonderful, however back at the base it was business as usual. The trip back was uneventful and a week off seemed just enough to re-charge the batteries. We were all anxious to get back to base and into our B-29's.

Since fresh pilots from the States did not have any combat time, they were taken from their crews, and reassigned as co-pilots with combat experienced crews. This was done in an effort to gain the experience needed to command a crew.

One particular experience that we had heard was that of one of these rookie co-pilots on a bombing mission to Singapore. This was a nine hour trip each way just to reach the target and something dreadful happened to this poor soul as the plane approached the target. From what we could piece together, the sky was full of enemy aircraft and a lot of flak (anti-aircraft artillery) and enemy fighters were all over the bomber. Supposedly, the plane was illuminated as enemy spot lights shined brightly on them as the anti-aircraft pelted the plane. The flak jostled the plane for a while, as they couldn't't get out of the flak field and as the pressure mounted, the inexperienced co-pilot had a sort of emotional breakdown. We had heard that the crew actually had to subdue him by tying him to his seat during this episode to prevent him from injuring himself. When his aircraft returned to the base, the officials grounded him for his actions. While we never heard anything about him after that, we assumed he had probably been hospitalized to recuperate. I hope that all went well with him, as I did know him personally, and he was a good guy.

Chapter VIII

Our First Combat Mission

With all this experience under our belts, or lack of it for better words, our first real mission took place on December 14, 1944. Most of us had a somewhat uneasy night, whether it be from the excitement of finally doing what we had been training for so long for, or the anxiety of realization in knowing that it's for keeps up there. We were awakened early, briefed as to what to expect, including the probability that we would encounter enemy fighters, and then dismissed. We were wished well by our briefing officers, and told to be on guard, but reassuringly told that we would be surrounded by experienced crews in the formation, and they would try to keep us out of harms way. Whether or not this was true, it seemed to take the edge off, at least slightly.

We would carry twelve 1,000 pound general purpose bombs and our target was the railroad yards in Bangkok, Thailand (French Indochina). We were to attack the Makkasan Railway workshops and yards in the area then called Burma. This being our first mission, we were all jumpy, to say the least.

Given time to grab some chow, I accompanied Shep to the mess hall to grab some breakfast.

"You hungry" Shep asked.

"Nah" I replied, feeling nauseous, I guess due to anxiety.

"Me neither," replied Shep as we both grabbed a cup of coffee, and a sweet roll.

We sat down together and neither of us had much to say, for that matter the mess hall was exceptionally quiet, as we would learn was the norm prior to a bombing mission. Everyone was quiet, alone, pondering thoughts of what was to come, deep in thought. I took one bite, gulped down the cup of coffee, and lit up a smoke and said to Shep

"That was the lousiest coffee I ever had"

"Yea has this distinct flavor of dirt" he replied.

"Come on, let's get going and catch up with the rest of the crew" I said.

We got to the plane early, and did all the mandatory prep work to insure our plane was ready, and boarded after the preliminary checklist, and protocol was completed. All systems checked out as we fired the engines, completed the balance of our checks, and began moving off the hard stand taxiing towards our place on the runway. Our plane was the Mary K, and we had flown her before on some training missions.

The bloated bomber lumbered down the runway, engines screaming as we gained speed .It was a cool morning for India, probably 95 degrees or so, and from my vantage point, I watched as the wings flex from the bumps on the runway until the bomber gracefully lifted from the ground. Our landing gear retracting, and the flaps retracted I reported to the pilot, and we were on our way.

"OK guys, everything looks good" the pilot reports over the inter-com.

Our trip was to be at least 9 hours till we reached the target, and in flying without fighter escort we stayed on alert as we made our way into enemy territory. The sweaty palms and difficulty swallowing were all as a result of our anxiety.

Were we ready? According to the Army Air Force we were. At our stations, everyone was alert searching the area for any signs of the enemy. The Briefing Officers had informed us that enemy planes would be in our area, so we searched the screen and the sky through the window blister diligently.

"Here comes one, left at ten o'clock high" Shep blurts out from his elevated stand.

Billie Frazier (left gunner) acknowledges enemy fighters coming in. He sets up, aligns the target and within seconds begins firing. He blurts out, "I'll get that SOB" in his typical Texas accent as the echo of the fifty caliber guns resonated within the plane. That first zero ducks under our plane,

"Your side now" he blurted out to me.

I already had a bead on him having tracked his approach and was getting ready to fire. I took over and gave that zero everything those fifties could deliver, but to no avail. It all happened so fast, and he flew out of range quickly and kept going.

"I tried to keep em' in the cross hairs, but he came in too fast" Billy said disappointedly.

"I missed him too, but at least he knows we're alert," I responded

Our tail gunner also had some action while we were getting to the IP when another enemy fighter tried a rear attack on us. The tail gunner let loose with some cannon fire on the unsuspecting Zero, this is all on our way in towards the drop zone.

Our initial point rendezvous or IP as it was called went without flaw, as we entered our slot in formation with the other bombers and made our way to the drop zone.

We had twelve, one thousand pound general purpose bombs in our belly, that we were about to drop on the target, which was a railroad bridge and as the bombardier took control of the plane, the tension mounted as we steady on our course. While the bombardier has control of the plane we are forced to fly at a constant speed, and altitude, and basically as straight as an arrow so our payload can be delivered to its intended destination. I diligently search the skies looking for any potential danger as we are at our most vulnerable state. We experience no enemy flak, but still there is the concern of those damn fighters, and it seems to be taking an exceptionally long time. I think to myself

"What's taking him so long, let's drop and get the hell out of here" as my thoughts are interrupted by the inter-phone.

"Bombs Away" …….. Oh, those sweet words came none to soon as the bomber lifts from expelling the four tons of explosives, and the bomb bay doors close and thereafter we make our turn and began heading for home. This was by no means indicative that we were out of danger at this point; it was just a progression of the routine that we would learn to face on an almost daily basis.

We still had to fly through the Hot Zone where we had engaged enemy fighters, so we were still alert, and on guard for the remainder of the trip home.

I don't know which was worse during the mission, whether it was those minutes over the target that felt like an eternity, or the nine hours it had just taken to get there, but here we were still facing an additional 8-9 hours or so just to get back to the base. This would take some getting used to.

Coming back from the mission we saw a B-29 from our group (the 468th) in trouble. We knew it was one of our group by the tail insignia, and with an engine lost; the pilot had feathered it, shutting the propellers so they don't rotate, causing drag. Apparently they had been shot up, and three zeros began attacking the plane.

I guess that they were under the impression that the crippled B-29 would be a sitting duck and an easy target to knock from the sky. The enemy made numerous attempts to knock down the plane but the defensive ability of the B-29 was phenomenal. Those fifty caliber machine guns were blazing at each turret and that twenty millimeter cannon in the tail pounded the enemy. The enemy fighters were out gunned, and no match for the Superfortress.

Cheering we watched on, as one by one the Zeros were knocked from the sky. What a great sight watching the enemies' planes being enveloped in smoke as they spiral downwards, smoke trails marking their decent. That is the type of fire power the B-29 had. It had just pummeled these enemy planes, while limping home, and in serious trouble itself.

During this ordeal, we were all pumped full of adrenaline and wanted to assist our comrades but strict regulations prohibited us from offering assistance to the crippled plane. We were over French Indochina, on the outskirts of Burma and knew that area was in the Japanese Empire's control. So if your plane ditched in that corridor it would be unlikely that you would return. I guess that's the logic the superiors used for reducing casualties in forbidding our assistance. For whatever reason, eight hours later the plane did successfully land at Kharagpur despite its lost engine and the damage it has sustained. We all gathered around and congratulated the crew.

This was our first experience with the enemy, and just prior to this mission, we were all given these small American flags that were the same size as handkerchiefs. They had writings in different languages on the back and we were instructed to keep them in our pockets and to use them in the event that we were shot down. All aircraft flying the southern route back to India were given them. The writings told any Allies that aid in our safe return to American personnel would result in a reward. That whole area was occupied by and under Japanese control. (I don't think there were too many allies there) with the exception of the Chinese Nationalists.

52

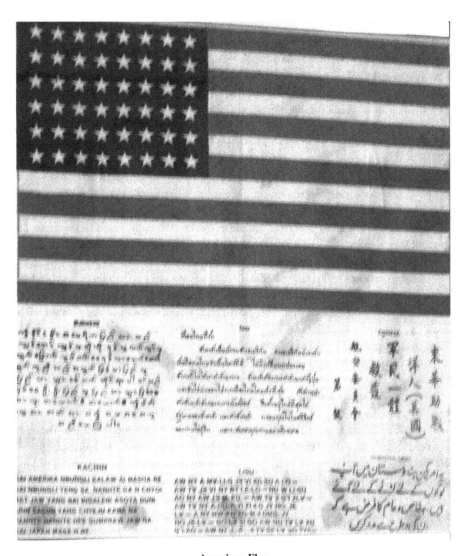

American Flag

The mission was no cakewalk, but then again none of them were. We all had heard rumors of some crews that had washed-out unable to withstand the pressures they were subjected to during combat, and of crewmen experiencing emotional breakdowns. I guess your first mission dictates the extent to which you handle things emotionally.

Our first mission was over we had survived and returned safely.

I guess we were ready or as ready as you can be under such circumstances. It's strange how first experience is the barometer to which all things are measured and compared. It was very scary and to this day I still have the occasional nightmare of that plane entering my field of vision and trying to shoot it down. I can truthfully say that I was so relieved that the zeros got out of there so quickly and didn't come back to bother us again.

As you have the ability to reflect later on in life, you become aware of all the possibilities of disaster you faced. Excluding the obvious combat damages, we were flying over enemy territory, flying over an ocean without any fighter escort. There were hours of flight that we saw nothing but the vastness of the ocean. Usually alone, we flew nine or ten hours to get to the target, the same number of hours to return. In that time you might experience any magnitude of variables that all meant trouble, or catastrophe. From engine failure, fire, oil leaks, hydraulic problems or explosion, any problem had the potential to put us in serious trouble. And with all these possibilities of disaster what were our options?

To ditch the plane at sea, bail out over the ocean, or to land in enemy territory. None of the options were pleasant, especially being that you had traveled significantly, just to hit the target. The thought of surviving an ordeal of that magnitude is frightening. Being our first mission, luckily we hadn't been subjected yet to severe atrocities, or been tainted emotionally by our fears.

After a day or so back on the base we heard of some of the hardships that other crews faced during that same mission. One in particular was of a West Point pilot that had his plane loaded with two different size bombs. This was not proper procedure, and the pilot was warned against doing this by the loading crew. The pilot pulled rank over the GI, and insisted that his plane be loaded the way he wanted. In the front bomb bay he had twelve 500 pounders loaded, and in the rear hatch, he insisted that six-1000 pound general purpose bombs be loaded. The 500 pounders were a new type that fused instantaneously, and packed with an extremely powerful but relatively unstable explosive.

They were in bombing formation and released the bomb load over the target when they were rocked by a mighty explosion. The bombs began exploding directly under the plane causing extensive damage to the bomber and other bombers that were in formation around it. That crew was forced to bail out of the plane and we later heard that they had been taken prisoner however there were others that were not so lucky. The other bomber crews behind them took direct hits to their bomb loads resulting in them exploding in mid air as a result of this mishap.

Reports of casualties to the media were only that of numbers of planes lost, never in the amount of lives lost. It is sad to think that each bomber represented eleven lives and how reports of these were never personalized by stating how many crew-members perished, only that a dozen of planes were lost. I guess that this was for wartime propaganda and lessening the demoralizing effect such news would have.

The very next day we were back in the saddle again flying a practice run that included additional training procedures and gunnery practice. During the next few days, we were kept busy with these same activities designed to more familiarize ourselves with the aircraft and our responsibilities. These included almost daily practice flights as procedures and practices from within the plane became routine. The exercises gave us an additional twenty hours of well needed flight time as we neared the Christmas holiday.

Back at the base on Christmas Eve we all were having a few drinks in celebration of the holiday, and to ease those typical holiday blues. We were all listening to Bing Crosby's new song,

54

White Christmas. I will never, ever forget that song and where I was at that time. Even today after sixty years, I became moved with emotion when hearing that song. There is nothing like it, I hear the music start and I'm transformed back in time and location to 1944. I recall there were drinks being served and I must have had a few and was feeling blue. My thoughts drifted thousands of miles from here, to a far nicer place and time that was shared with much better company. Not saying or even implying that the company I was with was bad, but when I closed my eyes, if only for those few seconds I was elsewhere, away from India, and the stresses of war. This little daydream had momentarily set me free of the drudgery and loneliness and put me back in a much more festive attitude about the holidays. I was happy and comfortable with this momentary lapse from the reality from this hell hole even though it was short lived, for my eyes re-opened quickly and widely due to the sudden break in the serenity. The ear piercing alarm of the Air Raid Sirens sounded, as the loud speakers blared;

"AIR RAID, TAKE COVER, AIR RAID."

In nano-seconds we are outdoors and jumping and diving into fox holes for cover. Just minutes before I had the visions of sugar plums dancing in my head, but not thirty seconds later I have my face buried in the dirt, and my concerns were no longer that of sugar plums dancing about, but of the reality of bombs raining down on my head and protecting myself from them.

A group of enemy fighters approach as the unmistakable sound of their presence near us. The Japanese fighters strafe the airfield as the resonating sound of gunfire and explosions fill the air. The ground pulsates from the concussion of the explosion as we lay helplessly in mother earth's arms, hoping that she will offer us protection, as the enemy continues to unload its wrath.

The attack only lasted a few minutes but in the darkness, it seems like hours. Even though I was face down with my eyes closed, I still saw the telltale flashes of light from the explosions and both heard and felt the explosion as the earth seemed to throb beneath me. An attack of this type is also an assault of your senses and your fears aren't't quelled until the All Clear signal blares. Even then, there is a reluctance to come out.

Anyway there ended up being no significant damage to our airfields and no B-29 had been hit. That episode however certainly brought me back to reality, and damn quick too. There is nothing like a shot of reality, to make you forget the blues, and to stop feeling sorry for yourself. There is something about scrambling into a foxhole, with adrenalin rushing, heart pounding, looking for cover to save your life, sort of puts things back into perspective.

In my opinion, the Japs sent those planes that night just because it was Christmas, in an effort to affect us psychologically, and they were surely successful in scaring us, but this also had another affect on us. It seems to have pissed us off just that much more and lead to a more cohesive bond between us. We would succeed in wreaking as much havoc as possible on this enemy that would be our revenge.

As a new crew, we were becoming slightly more seasoned with each completed mission under our belts. We all operated as a team and we were more attuned to procedures and protocol. We knew what to expect, when to expect it, and how to react to it. By the same token, when something wasn't right, we also knew about it.

_____

Chapter IX

Mission: Hump Trip into China

On December 29, 1944 we flew our second mission as we began ferrying bombs and fuel over the Himalayan Mountains, which we called The Hump into China. The Nationalist in China, under Cheng Kai-sheck had committed to aiding the allies by constructing airfields large enough to accommodate the Superfortress. This in turn would be used as a staging area for U.S. bombers to begin attacking the Japanese mainland. For the privilege of using these new air fields the U.S. government had paid Chang Kai-sheck handsomely.

There was no love between Japan and China and even though there was a political separation between the Chinese Communists and Chinese Nationalists, they both share a mutual hatred for the Japanese.

The Japanese had invaded Nanking, China in the mid 1930's and had committed atrocities against the Chinese people. They brutalized and butchered many innocent people, and still today there is animosity between them. It would become known in later years as the Rape of Nanking.

This was the first of such fields completed in China, and was now being used as a forward base or springboard for future bombing raids against the Japanese Empire. Our mission consisted of ferrying fuel and assorted bombs to stockpile an ample supply prior to the actual bombing mission. This was a major undertaking as each plane required a minimum of 7,000 gallons of fuel to hit Japan and there were to be at least 50 planes assigned to each mission.

On this particular flight there was a new pilot at the helm and our destination was Pengshan, China code name A7, located in central China's Szechwan Province. Our takeoff from India was without incident, and we were all becoming very comfortable with the routine, and our duties. Throughout the trip, we still were aware of the fact that enemy fighters could attack us at any time, so this mission was by no means a reprieve. The flight was a welcome change from the ever so oppressive heat of India. We had just crossed the treacherous Himalayas, a beautiful snow capped mountain range, yet one of the most dangerous parts of the trip, and within forty five minutes or so we would be landing at our destination. Our approach seemed routine as we neared the landing strip with our bloated bomber.

The pilot had engaged the landing gear, and was extending the flaps on the decent. Everyone reported back to the pilot, double checking with visual conformation as was routine as we neared the ground. The tension was beginning to ease as the first half mission would soon be over, and I began to relax for the first time in hours.

Suddenly, without warning the plane begins to climb, the engines growl back to life, howling as they were pushed to their maximum RPMS and we gain altitude quickly. I am immediately pinned back in my seat from the force of the plane, and fight to get up to my combat station. Reaching my station, while still getting my balance my immediate reaction was to jump to my guns and try to get a bead on whoever was attacking us. Everyone on the plane had sprung to their stations and we were ready for combat within seconds. Central Fire Control reported nothing, and both Tex and I searched both the sky, and the ground assessing the situation through the side blister windows and screens.

Himalayan Mountains

Within seconds the pilot announces on the intercom, sorry guys with a sheepish almost embarrassing tone, and proceeded to explain that we were not under attack, that he had simply overshot the airfield, and that we would be making another approach within a minute or so.

We all settled down.......... somewhat, .but now what entered my mind was concern about the pilots' ability to land. I think everyone had the same idea at the same time. We all knew only too well what the consequences were if we crashed, and there was a silence in the plane as I think we all quietly said a little prayer. We were loaded to capacity with additional canisters of aviation fuel, not to mention the bomb load in our Cache. If we'd crash landed we would have been engulfed in a fireball so hot that nothing of us would be left. Not that there is any good way to die, but perishing in a fireball that way seems to be the worst.

The second approach of the airstrip yielded considerably better results, we circled once and then finally made our approach and gracefully touch down coming to a stop on the newly constructed runway. The landing was perfect but it certainly took a while for our nerves to settle.

The Himalayan Mountain Range, while beautiful to see, was treacherous to fly over. The unpredictably volatile vertical drafts had caused many hardships and wreaked havoc on our planes. As a result, this placed us in constant jeopardy, and many B-29's were lost during these trips, while others fell victim to the menacing peaks attempting the crossing.

Excluding the dangerous up and down drafts, other factors such as human error, navigational or piloting miscalculations caused additional disasters. Now please remember that the B-29 was the first plane ever, to fly at such an altitude and there was no rule book to follow. The all-so familiar Jet Stream that we hear so much about today was discovered at this time. These planes were not following the rule books, but writing them, and as a result there were mishaps, casualties, and many of them.

B-29 with Camels

We all heard rumors of crews making it out of the plane after crashing over The Hump, but most perished trying to make it back to civilization. Those that were lucky enough to survive a crash faced unimaginable hardships. I have read accounts of starvation, no medical treatment, and months and months trying to elude capture by the enemy. These poor souls would have to stay on the move, fighting disease, starvation, and sickness, that most succumbed to in the end.

This flight time over the Himalayas was so dangerous, that we were given combat pay for each flight over the mountain range. This trip also counted as one of the thirty five missions required to complete before you were eligible for release from the Air Force. This is the reason you saw the camel markers on all early bombers in the CBI Theater, as they designated successful Hump Trips and were acknowledged for their involvement in these ferrying missions from India to China.

Anyway, after that nerve racking experience with landing, we exited the plane and left the unloading of the materials to the crews that manned the base. They would separate, and stockpile the munitions, and delegate the disbursement under the authority of the allies, as they saw fit. There were pursuit fighters that also shared this fuel and munitions.

I couldn't't help but notice a vile odor as the wind blew in our direction upon exiting the plane. It was cold out, and a welcome change of climate and it felt like December, back in the states.

"What the hell could have such a stench out here in the middle of nowhere" I asked. "It smells like good old Secaucus," an area back home that was laden with pig farms.

I looked around for a corral or pen that might be close by. There was nothing visible but rice patties on the very edge of the runway. The smell was revolting, and I finally asked someone about the vile stench. I was told that some of the trenches that looked like foxholes close to the base were also used for sewage, and to be careful of my choice of foxholes during an emergency.

"An error in judgment in using the drainage ditch instead of the foxhole could result in you being in a Crappy situation" I said as the group all laughed. We were told that it had happened more than once, and to be careful. Also that the stench issue was being rectified by the creation of military latrines, that were being constructed as we spoke.

We found the mess hall, and thankfully it was located on the other side of the base. The stench had diminished and was replaced with the smell of food being prepared, good food, or for that matter better than we had eaten in India, and no, it wasn't Chinese food either. We sat down to real food, and ate some dinner, and prepared ourselves for the next day's mission back to India. We had checked out the primitive barracks that we were to sleep in that evening, no electric, and a wood stove for heat, but it was no different than what we had become used to. However the difference in climate seemed somewhat refreshing after having been subjected to India. It was still early enough in the day to see the sights of the area.

I had seen a nearby village on our first approach of the landing strip; we passed right over it, and were close enough to see the activity from above. It was within walking distance of the base so a group of us decided to see what was happening there. We walked towards the village when, from behind a Chinaman pulling a rickshaw caught up to us and began verbalizing something at us. We had no idea what he was saying, and although it sounded like he was screaming at us, he motioned at us to hop in.

"No that's OK, we'll walk" I said shaking my head.

He wouldn't take no for an answer, and again began the gibberish, and louder than before, as a few of his cronies pulled up right behind him, all anxious to chauffeur us.

"Hey guys, I guess we're going to ride to the village" comes a response from the back so we all hopped in, two at a time for the ride.

"I hope the villagers don't think we're millionaires, being driven up in these Hansom carriages" I said to Shep.

"Oh yea, they'll probably raise the price of everything, but what the hell, I'm not buying anything" he replied.

We paid the guy, and while no one knew what to pay him, or for that matter what the hell he was saying, but we reached a happy medium as the Chinaman bowed and smiled continuously.

The Chinese people were very hospitable to American fliers and were anxious to sell whatever they could to us. This was an open air market that sold everything imaginable.

One particular booth must have been a butcher shop as there was some kind of cured meat that they had hanging outside, as we passed the merchant saw me looking and rushed to me as a potential customer.

"Hey Nick, this guy wants you to taste that," Shep said to me.

The merchant had already broken off pieces and was offering it to me.

"No, no thanks," I said trying not to hurt the guys feelings,

"What the hell is this guy offering me," I didn't know what kind of meat it was, and graciously passed on their generosity.

"Come on Nick" I heard from someone behind me "Give it a try."

I had heard of some strange cuisine in that part of the world, and didn't have the urge or desire to try. For all I knew that could have been monkey meat or dog, or something of the sort, and I had no desire to Broaden my Horizons with this type of exotic culinary cuisine. It also didn't appear to be too sanitary, so I just smiled and continued on hastening my step a bit.

From homemade cooking pots to useful hand crafted items and even some Chinese antiquities these people tried to sell us anything. There was one big problem, none of us spoke the language or for that matter knew what we were looking at. The more the merchant tried to persuade us into a purchase, his enthusiasm and zeal made him speak faster and louder in an effort to convince us.

"I don't know if the guy was getting pissed off at me" I said, so I incorporated the universal language when dealing with the merchants. A smile and a nod yes, or a head shake from side to side no was the usual extent of our communication. The only saying that I remembered there was Ding How, what I believe to be some sort of greeting.

Anyhow it was nice to see the crowds of people there on the streets and seeing how different, yet surprisingly similar people of different cultures are. The range of age in the village was from small children to very elderly and the young children would gaze at us with eyes as big as silver dollars. Whether it was our uniforms or just the fact of seeing someone who looked different, but these children were always smiling. It was a welcome change to be outside of the heat of India and to see another culture's daily life.

We went back to the base for the evening and spent the balance of our time preparing for the return trip the next morning. With nothing better to do, we got involved in a poker game with a few crew members. It was always a friendly game, usually with the same nickel a hand ante, most often just to pass the time.

With kerosene lanterns illuminating our playing table the game had been on for an hour or so, and our tail gunner had won just about every hand. This guy was smoking that night, he certainly had a knack for the game, either he was very lucky or a very skilled at the art of deception. He convinced us to raise the ante in an effort to increase the size of the pot and his rally. He had been on fire with luck for the majority of the evening, and had been watching him closely, and saw no signs of wrong doing in his game but the tables were about to turn. I finally landed a killer hand and was in the process of recouping my losses and then some. I had to play it right, as I didn't want to seem over anxious, so I stayed calm and played the hand with my emotions in check.

I remembered my friends from Miami, old Frankie, and Joey, and played the hand like a pro.

"Yea, I'll take one card," I said, as I discarded and shook my head in a theatrically disappointing manner.

As the pot swelled, I could taste the sweetness of winning that swollen pot, but still played casually.

We were on the last call of the hand, everyone had folded but the tail gunner, myself, and one other person, and I soon felt it would be read'em and weep, boys. The tension of the game and the stillness of the night was interrupted by the Air Raid Siren alarm, as the loudspeaker blared "Take Cover, Air Raid."

We immediately scrambled for cover, leaving the cards, the money, everything on the table, as we ran outside. The base went dark as some of us dove into, and others groped their way into foxholes or other makeshift areas for cover. First and foremost was remembering the right ditch to be in, but luckily I'd made the right choice.

During an Air-Raid all lights are extinguished, in an effort to stay hidden from the enemy. Any light, no matter how small can be seen from the sky, and creates a target for which the enemy can aim.

Before the impending strike there is chaos during the few seconds as you brace for the coming bombardment. Someone spots one of the coolies smoking a cigarette out in the open and motions to him to get down on the ground and to put out the cigarette. Either this guy didn't know what an Air-Raid siren was, or was working for the Japanese as a spy.

"Someone grab that guy" I heard as I settled into the trench.

He calmly stayed out in the open deeply puffing away, the embers of the cigarette brightened with every puff, oblivious to the warning.

"Put out the cigarette" someone yells from the foxhole as more of us become aware of what's happening. An increasing numbers of shouts begin to emerge from all areas, as the coolie becomes the central point of focus, and all eyes shift towards him. His actions are putting us all in grave danger, as we hear the Jap fighter planes nearing us.

"That idiot is going to get us killed I overhear from the side area. The enemy is now seconds away from striking distance as a panic overcomes us. We are all armed with our shoulder 45s, so no one will ever know for sure what happened.

A group of six fighters strafe the field laying down a path of machine gun fire that resonated all around us. The pitch of their engines' and the zip of the bullets flying past are clearly unnerving. My face is buried in the ground as the onslaught continues. I heard the muted whistle of bombs being dropped, increasing in intensity as they neared me. I brace for the impact, covering my head, and protecting my ears with my hands. The crash of the explosion shakes the ground on impact as bits of earth and iron fragments come raining down all over me... the other blasts follow, although with less intensity... and then, .the moment passes. I feel no physical pain, other than the ringing in my ears, and the damn humming noise that goes along with it, yet I see no blood, that's a good sign. I don't know if they are going to make another swoop at us so I stay down.

Suddenly it's all quiet... an eerily silence for what seems to be too long..... the only sound I can hear is the thumping of my heart, pounding in my chest like a bass drum, it sounds so loud that I'm sure the guy next to me can hear it, ... finally the all clear signal blares.

As quickly as it begins, it is over, and I slowly emerge, cautiously raising my head from hiding.

The first sight that captures my eye when the smoke cleared was the Chinese peasant, he lay motionless, face down, still holding the remnants of a burnt out cigarette in his hand.

We'll never know if it was a GI's 45 slug that killed him, or the enemy machine gun fire. We got up, dusted ourselves off, and made an assessment of the area.

Damage to the base was minimal and our plane had fared well. The Chinese had employed a type of homemade camouflage on our plane, and although it was parked close by, it had remained obviously hidden from the view. They had ingeniously used whatever was available to hide the plane, primarily tree branches, mud, bark and dirt and had successfully hidden it from above.

The runway had taken a hit from one of the bombs, but that would be easily repaired in time for our take off. While I can't remember what ever happened to the poker winnings, most of us were preoccupied with why there were no anti-aircraft guns in place, and if we would be in constant jeopardy from Japanese held positions in China.

We notified the authorities that one of the Chinese peasants had been killed, and also of his strange behavior prior to the assault. Emphasis was put on the fact that this type of activity had jeopardized our safety, and would not be tolerated.

Hiding B-29 in China

Chapter X

Construction in China

With only one airstrip completed in Pengshan, the Nationalists were busy fulfilling the commitment of building additional runways and construction was underway at the time of our first landing. As we neared this construction project to get a better view of it's progress and their technique for building, there seemed to be a great deal of shouting going on, which is usually the case when you don't understand the language.

The labor force was massive, and from what we saw there was no machinery being used at all, not even any animals to help haul materials. This entire project was to be accomplished in the most primitive and physical manner imaginable. This massive undertaking began with the labor force digging up large rocks, breaking them with a sledge hammer to make a sort of gravel. Upon completion the crushed stone was then shoveled into straw baskets to be transferred to the runway. This was accomplished by each person balancing two baskets attached to a yoke that was placed over the neck and shoulders as they then physically walked to the runway to dump the contents.

An elderly male supervised by instructing where to dump the crushed stone as this process continued endlessly. As the supervisors guided the laborers, I was shocked to see that it was mostly women that were performing this physical labor. The few men that were visibly working acted so primarily in a supervisory capacity; the majority of the workers were women. I guess it stood to reason that the majority of the men were in the Chinese Army, either fighting the Chinese Communists, or the Japanese that had invaded China and had control of major sections.

The next process of the construction consisted of flattening the gravel by use of a large roller either made of concrete, or some other quarried stone that was 12 foot wide and 8 foot in diameter. It had a large hole in the center where a tree trunk had been inserted that protruded about 4 or 5 feet on either side. Ropes had been attached to these protruded sections of the tree trunk, and thousands of laborers would then pull the immense roller with nothing more than the strength of their backs. It is unbelievable that the momentum gained by this large flattening stone, as it must have weighed a few tons. I am sure there were many fatalities as a result of the inability to control that large rolling pin. This process was surprisingly effective in completing the task of flattening the runway, making it smooth enough to be used as a runway. This is a sight that I will never forget; such a labor force completing monumental tasks that I had only seen done by machinery was unbelievable to watch.

Construction in China

The end process was the coolies then pouring some sort of oil onto the flattened runway that had the effect of solidifying the amalgam, and sealing it.

The Chinese people did everything by hand, with backbreaking sweat and toil with labor pools ranging in the hundreds of thousands of people. If you think back historically, this was the same technique that must have been employed to construct the Great Wall of China hundreds of years prior, and other monumental tasks completed before the mechanized 20th century.

There were additional bases built in China that were ultimately built to accommodate the bases that were stationed in India. They were, Kwangham, Chengtu, Kiunglai, and of course Pengshan, the base that housed our squadron, the 468th Bomb Group. America would use all these bases in China on every trip we made to bomb the Japanese Empire, therefore all the Chinese bases needed to be supplied. The Chinese Nationalists would aid us in any capacity with camouflage, and would stand guard overnight, although I do recall that we also stood guard on a rotating schedule for the extent of time that we were there. There were absolutely no hangers at A7, so all repair work was done out in the open.

It soon became obvious to our leaders that these bases in China had limitations. While succeeding in giving the Allies the ability to strike Japan, the difficulties lay in supplying the Chinese bases from India, and the inaccessibility of alternate means of supply.

Had there been access to a shipping supply route, which could possibly have eased the supply burden, might have been the answer; however there was no easy fix. The Japanese were still aggressively active in China, which still posed another threat. We would need a closer area, if we were to continue with the plans for increasing both the frequency and the ferocity of attacks on the Japanese Empire.

We had become a team and there became a certain bond between us that only can be explained as a brotherhood that we shared with each other. There is one particular incident that comes to mind that exemplifies this brotherhood. There was an unwritten law on our plane, that whoever used the portable toilet first had to empty it when we landed back at the base. We all suffered from some sort of stomach ailments on most missions, and I guess it wasn't that big a deal, however this particular day I had been the first to use it and there were many more crew members that used it afterwards.

Dreading the prospects of that loathsome trip to the latrine to dump it, I got this brilliant idea that I thought would save me the trip.

Being that we were pressurized, my logic deduced that if I empty the waste canister into the camera hatch, it would be sucked right out, sheer brilliance I thought. The slot is big enough, and will draw this stuff right out, so we were flying at eight thousand feet, coming close to home when I decided to put my idea into practice. I grabbed the canister, walked into the camera hatch area, unobserved and then began pouring the contents of the toilet down the hatch. All went well as I sort of guided the waste with my head turned, without really looking at the vile contents.

Man, this worked well I said to myself as the majority was expelled and the canister lightened. I was kind of proud of myself for what I perceived to be a stroke of genius, as I sat there gloating. I started laughing that some unsuspecting soul walking below was going to get a shit shower, and laughing to myself said I hope he is carrying an umbrella, when the unthinkable happened.

We hit a wind backlash that interrupted the Glug-Glug sound, and then I heard a swish and some of the contents began to blow back into the plane. I quickly moved to get out of the way, and as I did I looked back at the bulkhead area, and to my horror, there was covered with the remnants of the waste I had dumped. Luckily, none had blown back in my face, but I was in trouble.

"What the hell stinks" comes from the rear compartment.

"Man, that smells so bad I can almost taste it …Whew, Nick is that you" came another comment.

I stepped out of the semi-private area that housed the latrine canister, nervously giggling.

"Oh wow guys, I'm sorry," I said and proceeded to tell the crew what I had done.

"Lucky we'll be landing in about 5 minutes" said Shep his face distorted from the stench, grabbing the emergency oxygen canister and covered his face.

We landed, and as soon as the plane came to a stop, all hatches flow open, and everyone exited with the speed of an emergency.

By this time, the whole plane reeked; it was ripe in that back compartment. The ground crew came in and ran out again, "Holly Cow, what the hell happened in there?" they asked holding there noses.

"Defective toilet" one of our crew shouted out.

"Don't you guys check this stuff out before we fly" posing the question to the ground crew," You guys better get on the ball."

The plane was grounded for close to two weeks as it was fumigated and thoroughly cleaned.

The entire crew knew what I had done but no one spoke about it or said anything. No one knew anything about it when questioned. The major consensus was that it must have been a Defective Toilet. I thought for sure that the Commanding Officer would be calling me in for a reprimand, but it never happened. I was lucky, no one spoke a word about it and I never did that stupid maneuver again.

One of the most respected officers in our command was the late Lt. Gen. James V. Edmundson part of our briefing personnel. He was a thin seasoned officer with a gravely voice that sported a pencil thin moustache and would always be chomping on a cigar. He shared the intelligence that had been gathered with us about the target we were to hit. He briefed us as to what we would encounter, as he showed maps and gave tactical advice.

"Ok men, this is what we are up against today" was his usual opening as I recall, "and this is how we're going to accomplish it," and with the mannerism of a football coach, and the bravado of a warrior he would draw diagrams of the play and unfold it to his team.

He was beloved to the flyers for his motto was, I would never ask you to do something that I would not do. He would accompany our group on many missions, flying in the lead B-29 over the target, a real hands-on type of leader. This man had a set of brass nuggets and was fearless, truly a great role model and leader.

Tokyo Rose, the despicable diva of the Japanese airwaves was privy to secret information, and at one time aired that the Japanese Empire had placed a bounty on the head of Edmundson of $10,000 American Dollars, Dead or Alive. Now that was a whole lot of money at the time but unfazed, he would be there every mission, reviewing the forthcoming procedures and giving advice. The crews, so revered him, because his attitude and actions were not that of a superior, but one of us. As a result, all his crews gave 110%. His actions and attitude had a huge psychological impact on us all.

It wasn't until General Curtis LeMay as Commander of the 20th Air Force forbid Edmundson to make any additional flights, did he stop flying, and that was only on direct orders. He will always be regarded as a great man, and with his recent passing he is well remembered. It was both an honor and privilege to have served with him.

Tokyo Rose, was a detestable wench who was privileged to an awful lot of information that was sometimes of disturbing proportions. She would interrupt the radio station and in an American voice, spread propaganda of Anti-American sentiment. I refused to even listen to her B.S., so as soon as the radio program was interrupted, I shut it off. She had access to information such as the insignias on new planes that had just landed and of new crews, all designed to intimidate the American Flyers.

"I'd like to welcome the new units of the 58th to the area," and she began to mention names, planes and codes numbers that these groups were flying in, as part of her propaganda statements.

I did find out that she was incarcerated after the war and was imprisoned for a while.

President Gerald Ford pardoned her in 1977 but she maintained her innocence, stating there had been many persons airing propaganda against the U.S. The term Tokyo Rose was an American made name, and that she had never aired anything by that name. Her objective was one of assistance, not encumbrance to America. Other than some coded types of messages designed to assist America, she played no role in the airing of propaganda.

Chapter XI

New Orders Regarding Bombing Procedures

As stated earlier, the B-29 was designed and implemented as a high altitude precision bomber, with the ability to fly at 30,000 feet or higher if necessary. While beneficial to fly at higher altitudes for the obvious reason of safety for the crew, the bombardiers found it difficult to spot targets clearly on the ground at the higher altitudes. This was due to the fact that blinding cloud cover and overcast conditions shrouded most target areas. This part of Asia has very unpredictable weather and was subject to fast moving weather fronts that would impede visibility conditions and thus influence the degree of success or failure of the mission. This altitude gave the American fliers their first experiences with the intensity of the then unfamiliar jet streams and learning to maneuver within them was on a trial and error basis. Flying at about five and a half miles high caused additional problems such as sudden wind shifts that could shift the plane off course so with all of these variables there were many times that we were unable to completely wipe out the targets on the first mission. As a result, it became common for us to return additional times to fully destroy the target.

Sometime in late 1944 our new Commanding Officer, General Curtis LeMay came aboard from the European theater. Germany was on the threshold of defeat so General LeMay's expertise was switched from Europe to the CBI Theater. Upon taking over and analyzing the efficiency and effectiveness of our bombing runs, he concluded that change was needed.

After much analysis he determined that the deficiency lay in the altitude at which we conducted our bombing raids. We would be much more effective in the destruction of targets if the assault were done at a lower altitude. However beneficial this change to the effectiveness would prove to be, the results might also prove disastrous in the loss of many more aircraft, and American lives. He knew that this modification would meet with steep opposition from the crews, and supposedly spent much time analyzing other alternatives, but ultimately determined that this modification was the right thing to do. The implementation would greatly increase the effectiveness of all bombing runs, and thus shorten the war.

At the next briefing we were informed of the new orders, and were instructed from this day forward, that all combat units are to fly between 8,000 and 12,000 feet on all bombing runs, including daylight missions.

This decision did not go over well at all with the bomber crews, because it put us at a much greater risk. Flying at a lower altitude would make us much more susceptible to enemy flak and an easier target for being shot down. This decision caused much dissension within the ranks as we argued among ourselves on what, if any advantage this new maneuver would have. However, we were still in the service and had no option other than to obey the new orders.

"8000 feet, this guy has no regard for our lives" blurted a shout from the back of the room. The rest of the room shared the sentiment.

"That's insane, I want to get home alive" vocalized another shout from the back.

"We're going to be flying 8,000 feet over Hell" I said to Shep.

"You're not kidding 8000 feet over Hell" he repeats

The bickering and groaning finally stopped after a few missions and our track record improved drastically. We began destroying the targets completely, the first time, every time, as the constricting noose around Japan's neck began to tighten.

Chapter XII

Mission:
Mukden, Manchuria

On January 3ʳᵈ, 1945 we were assigned our next mission, the destruction of Mukden, Manchuria from our base in China. This city was the steel producing giant of Communist China and had been in control of Japan since 1937 during the invasion of Manchuria. There were aircraft factories, rail yards and enemy arsenals that were both primary and secondary targets.

We rose early followed the usual protocol of being briefed, getting breakfast, and had done all preliminary setup and inspection outside the plane. We had boarded and were in the process of completing our preliminary checks, and began running through our pre-flight check lists. Our Engineer's examination of the instrument panel showed a problem with oil pressure with our #1 engine, and after double checking the instrument panel for the possibility of a malfunction of the gauge, he reported the problem to the pilot. This, in its self was cause to abort the mission for mechanical reasons even before takeoff, and it was decided to have the problem rectified, and abort the mission. Our engineer was the oldest of the lot and took his position very seriously, as we all did, but as not to jeopardize our safety the call to abort the mission was the right thing to do. To this dedication we owe a debt of gratitude and this in conjunction with everyone doing their job properly, do we owe the good fortune of our return. Our record at the end of the war would be only two aborted missions out of the thirty five. The ground crews were good mechanics and kept our planes in good working order.

Protocol dictated that when a mission was aborted, the crew stayed with the plane until the bomb squad arrived. We stayed within the vicinity of the plane until all bombs were removed from their racks within the bomb bays, and ammunition stowed. At that point we were transported back to our barracks.

On Jan. 4ᵗʰ through the 5ᵗʰ we ferried both bombs and fuel from our base in India to China making that terrible trip over the Hump. Trips over and back were uneventful, but took about 6 and a half hours each way.

On January 8ᵗʰ thankfully we were sent on a practice mission for bombing and gunnery practice to Halliday Island where we had been many times. We thought that we might be able to sink that little uninhabited island with the amount of lead and bombs we had thrown at her. January 13th and 14th again saw us participating in the stockpiling effort for fuel and ammo on that trip from India to A-7 China. The stockpile had grown sufficiently so we knew that soon we would be flying combat mission. This flight required the same 6 and a half hour routine both there and back.

Chapter XIII

Mission:
Bombing Raid; Formosa

On January 16, 1945 we left India in preparation for an attack on Formosa (Taiwan) the next day. We flew over The Hump and landed at one of the newly constructed runways in A7 China. It felt good in knowing that we would be using some of that fuel and bombs that we had been ferrying for so long, on the enemy for which it was intended. There was an air of apprehension throughout the flight, not spoken, but nevertheless there.

We got to China quickly by comparison, had landed and were in preparation for the early morning rise to be briefed. The Chinese soldiers were responsible for guarding our B-29's as we retired early in the evening in the Spartan barracks.

Having been asleep for less than an hour, the Air Raid signal goes off in the middle of the night as we wake and groggily scramble for cover. The place is pitch dark, as I heard the incoming fighters making there way towards us.

"Boy, this is becoming a habit, what's going on here" said Shep

"Where are the anti-aircraft guns that we were told would be here" I questioned There still were no guns and from my vantage point, but I noticed a larger problem unfolding.

"What's that...... look at that..... over there" I said noticing a small fire ignite alongside the runway,......... than another, ...and still another.

"Oh my god, this is no accident, these are signal fires and we have got a serious problem" I said. "We'll be sitting ducks this close to the runway."

The Chinese Nationalists ran towards the fires and extinguished them quickly, stomping the burning embers out with their boots. Luckily they were snuffed out before the enemy planes came within range, so they did not have a reference point to drop their bomb loads, thankfully.

The planes zipped by us without dropping their loads on us, seemingly waiting for the signals that never came, and in a few minutes the all clear alarm went off and we exited from hiding. Obviously there had been a security breach and as we returned to our barracks I was puzzled at the lack of defense on this base, and again the risk that it put us in. We talked about having the ability to get into our plane and at least be able to defend ourselves in case of another attack, but from what I was to find out, the search for the responsible parties had begun.

. In the early morning hours, approximately 4 A.M. we were awakened, and prepared for that day's mission. Our briefing included the usual information, the IP (initial point) rendez-vous, altitude, and formation, essentially what to expect from the enemy. In addition, we were also told that the responsible parties for the signal lighting from the previous evening had been captured. The Nationalists had obviously pursued these traitors relentlessly throughout the night, and ultimately found the guilty parties, and imposed their own justice upon them. I could imagine the severity of the punishment, however the details were sketchy. I think I overheard something about them hanging by the thumbs, but the details were never made clear to us.

At 7:30 a.m. January 17th 1945 we took off for the target, Formosa, then controlled by Japan. This would be a daylight mission, and estimated time of IP was 12:00 noon. We were flying the Bell- A-bortion carrying 27 500- pound general purpose bombs. The entire crew was unusually tense with the prospects of this mission. We all knew the reason yet no one dare even mention one word of why. Superstition played a major role in how many of the crew members handled the stresses of combat and while no one really believed in it, we all knew the role luck played, and above all, we wanted to be lucky. There were no horse shoes or rabbits feet, but no one wanted to jinx the mission.

We all sat there at our stations doing the jobs that we had been trained to do, in a comfort-able climate, yet beads of sweat trickled down my forehead. My eyes searched the sky look-ing for enemy fighters as I tried not to think about the anxiety. The hours slowly ticked away, minute by minute, with each elapsing second bringing us closer to the target, and the closer we got, the more anxious I felt. The rest of the crew was just as anxious, as there was much less conversation than normal. What strange thoughts and worries go through your mind?

Logical or not, the reason for all this worry and superstition was that originally, when we were assigned as Crew # 70, we were designated a replacement crew for one that had been shot down. We were replacing the original Crew 70 that was shot down over Formosa. Here we were, in the very spot that the first crew met its demise.

Whether rational, or not, was this the omen that would be the cause of our undoing? Nervously, we passed the IP, and entered our slot in the bombing formation, we were unde-tected thus far. The target in sight, bomb bays wide open, and the tension could be cut with a knife. The bombardier had total control of the plane, as everyone, wide alert at their positions, was poised to spring into action. Flak suits and helmets on, I search the skies as our bomb load is expelled, the Bombs Away alert sounded and we quickly descend into a turn that would lead us home.

Anti-aircraft bombs begin bursting around us in a wide array of colors and depth of sound. We had gotten in undetected and had obviously committed some serious damage on the en-emy, and now they wanted revenge. We inched our way through the barrage of fire, though the turbulence that jolted the plane and the horrible ack-ack sound of exploding antiaircraft fire around us. Minute by minute we flew, changing altitude in an effort to get out of range of the antiaircraft guns.

Our defense strategy worked as the onslaught seemed to dwindle and ultimately stop. We had made it and were out of the danger area of the target zone. The trip back to A7 was uneventful but we still kept a watchful eye in the skies as we neared the base in China. There was always the problem with fuel consumption, and the fear of running out, and this being a 10 hour trip was additional stress on the nerves of the haggard crew.

Our landing was perfect, and after the usual routine of stowing our gear, and shutting and securing all of our equipment we made our way to be debriefed on what we saw. After having a shot or two of whiskey that was always present at these debriefings, the whole crew retired for the evening, exhausted from the stresses of the day.

The next morning after breakfast in the base, we refueled and preceded to transverse the Himalayas to our home base in India. This ended up being a 6 hour trek and we were particularly watchful for any rogue enemy fighters as we crossed the Mountain Range.

Someone spots a plane in front of us, it's a fighter, as we begin analyzing its markings as we tracked it, while still searching the skies for any additional fighters.

It turns out that he is one of ours, a P-38 pursuit plane (very fast) crossing The Hump into India. We made contact with him, and began closing the distance between us.

"It looks like we're going to pass him," said Shep from his elevated position.

"What are you crazy" blurts out Tex, "That fighter could eat us for dinner" he asserts.

Now Tex was right, that in being a pursuit plane, it was capable of flying much faster than we could.

"We're gaining on him now, care to wager" says Shep

"Now that's a sucker bet, this guy might be conserving fuel, or maybe he's been shot up, my momma didn't raise no fool," Tex replied

I sat there, shaking my head and smiling.

Tex had always been sort of a hot head, and Shep always found humor in pushing his buttons, not belligerently, just enough to needle him. They both got along, and seemed to have a decent, but odd relationship.

"How about the tail winds, maybe they might have something to do with it" I interject trying to stay neutral in the conversation.

There were great southern tail winds in that area, that did help propel our plane, and we did catch up to, and ultimately pass the P-38. The most likely explanation was our large surface area, in reaction to the winds, but what ever the reason, it was fun to pass him. It was a nice break from the reality and with the anguish we had been through the day before, it relieved some of the stress. We made it home unscathed, thank God.

With the frequency of our trips to China, increasing our exposure to the culture, we became aware of some oddities and strange beliefs of its people. The Chinese peasants had this odd superstition that from birth they were plagued by an evil dragon that followed them in their shadow. This creature brought them terribly bad luck as it followed them, and at all times they sought a way to rid themselves of this menacing evil. Now we all know that a shadow is created by blocking the sun light, but yet this belief was part of ancient Chinese lore.

The sight of the B-29's spinning propellers' seemed to be an answer to the problem of the evil dragon. The people began to walk extremely close to the swirling propeller blades in hopes that the wicked dragon would be slain by the spinning props, and they would be freed. Of course this did not happen and those who got too close were killed in the most atrocious manner. Countless Chinese peasants perished during these propeller startups and it was a horrible thing to witness. Apart from the gore of these incidences, they would also cause great damage to our propellers and the frequency of occurrence began being viewed as delaying the war effort. Our desensitized Commanding Officers became frustrated with this unnecessary delay and issued orders preventing the peasants from coming close to the planes during startups. These orders were carried out by the Nationalists and they showed little tolerance for any offenders.

These same Nationalists who were left guarding our supplies and planes would often show us wads of American greenbacks hinting they were eager to buy American products from us. They loved American cigarettes and after smoking a Chinese one in a trade, I knew why! It was like smoking rolled horse shit.

Obviously there was a black market for American smokes; I was naive to it in the beginning. I recall I went to the PX and purchased a carton of cigarettes for $1.00 and was walking back when approached by a Chinese soldier with a $20.00 bill. He motioned that he would like the cigarettes and slipped the twenty into my hand for the smokes. I figured what the hell, that's a lot of money, but later my conscience got the best of me for doing this. I felt sorry for these poor people and I didn't want to take advantage of them.

I never did that again, but spoke to some friends about it. They quickly brought to my attention that there was a black market for American goods; they had done some of it also, but that the process was illegal.

On January 22, we flew a test hop of a bomber that had some modifications done to it. If I recall the plane had been converted to lay down mines, so its bomb bays housed a type of mechanism designed to drop mines without detonating them. We were ordered to take it for a test flight of three hours, I guess to get a feel for the plane. We completed our mission, and spent the rest of the day relaxing for the next day's mission.

Chapter XIV

Mission:
Mining Singapore

Early in the war's progression, the Japanese had captured Singapore from the English. Singapore had been in English control for many years and as a result had installed the latest type of antiaircraft artillery. The primary use of these weapons was defending the Singapore dry docks. These guns were very accurate, utilizing the latest technology and were now in the hands of the enemy. This area had always been a hot spot with the enemy inflicting heavy damage on us and most fliers were a little apprehensive about going there. We would soon see just what those guns would deliver.

On January 25th and 26th, 1945 we would face the onslaught of these enemy guns first hand. Our mission was to mine the approaches into the Straights of Singapore. This was done in an effort to stop supplies from reaching Japan. Without fuel and food the enemy is unable to continue its war effort. We had all heard the rumors of such accuracy of their guns in and about the area but still our mission was clear.

Now you can't help but get caught up in the hype, especially when it's your crew on the line, so needless to say, we were apprehensive of this mission. We were awakened that evening/early morning, and our old friend, Lt. Gen. Edmundson was right there briefing us on what to expect and how to elude problems. That in itself somehow took the edge off. He smiled and said he would see us back the next day. We were given strategic points at which to drop our mines, which included time allocations for perfect positioning. This would be a 9 hour trek to reach the target and the same amount of hours for the return trip. We would be alone for the entire trip and had our belly loaded with 6 - 1,000 lb mines as we took off from our base in India.

We flew over water for the entire trip and saw nothing of the enemy. When you have been in combat for a while you sort of get this sixth sense. You can't exactly put your finger on what it is but you have this feeling. If there is nothing happening, you're worried. On the other hand, you're also concerned about being attacked. So in essence, you're worried all the time.

"I hope those guns aren't't as accurate as we're lead to believe," I say to Shep

"We'll be all right, he knows what to do," he replies, referring to the pilot.

My mind races constantly as I try to keep my nerves in check. We are expected to reach the target at 6:30 A.M. that meant only half an hour left. Everything was in place and we were ready. The trip there went without incident, seemingly almost too easy.

We made our approach low and began the task of delivering the mines. I could hear the muffled splash as the first mine hit the water. The small parachutes on each mine deployed after ejection slowing the rate of fall, preventing detonation on impact. Within 4 minutes we had dropped all six mines and were on our way home. We stayed low under enemy radar, dangerously low, and this would be our M/O until we thought we were far enough away from Singapore.

"Where the hell is everyone, was last night Japanese New Years" came a voice from the inter-com.

"Maybe it's Sunday morning and everyone's gone to church," I replied chuckling.

"All right we've got activity near the dry docks, enemy running to man the Big Guns," reports tail gunner to pilot.

"Stand ready, we might have some company" reports the pilot, but within minutes we were well out of range. Surprisingly no fighter aircraft were deployed.

Our flight home was without incident; however we still diligently searched the skies for enemy fighters but were never challenged.

Chapter XV

Mission:
Raid on Alorstar, Malaysia

During the next few days we made a few test hop flights for a total of about 7 hours of flight. February 19th was our next combat mission for a raid on Alorstar, West Malaysia. We carried eight 1,000 lb general purpose bombs and were ordered to drop them over the targeted rail yard. This was a long and grueling mission that took 16 hours to complete. We flew in formation and blasted the target without any opposition. This target had been occupied by the Japanese since the bombing of Pearl Harbor, and was noted for being a hot-spot for enemy fighters. We were on guard and ready, but were never engaged by enemy fighters.

Chapter XVI

Mission:
Raid on Singapore

On March 1st our orders were to fly a bombing run in daylight formation mission to Singapore at 12,000 feet. We were pleased with the orders noting that our altitude placed us above most other planes, and awarded us a sense of security. We carried eight 500-pound bombs and reached the IP and got into formation at the proper time and altitude. The mission seemed to be going well, we had seen no defensive action taken by the Japanese and as we merged into the slot and approached the target we noticed that there were a few B-29's above us.

"What the hell are those guys doing" Shep blurts out from his stand. He immediately calls the pilot and explains the situation.

"They're dropping their loads" I scream as the sight of falling bombs tumble past my blister window. Now began the barrage of shells that rained down upon us, some missing us by mere inches, as we held our breath and prayed that Lady Luck was with us. We were directly beneath them as we watched in horror as these bombs whirled by us.

It was over in about 12 seconds, and I have to be honest, my eyes were closed, and I thought it was time to meet my maker. We had been on Auto-pilot, and had also expelled our load at the same time. I don't know if that saved us, or we were just lucky, damn lucky.

"Let's shoot those bastards down," Tex grabs his sights and tries to get a bead on the rogue bomber.

"How could those guys be so stupid, their bombardier surely must have seen we're American bombers beneath him" says Shep.

"Try to get the SOB's numbers or at least the insignia on the tail" I yell out, but all efforts are futile, and the guilty bombers disappear from our sight.

Apparently the high flying planes feared the assault of the big guns and had deliberately disobeyed General LeMays orders on the specified altitude of the drop.

This was a direct violation, punishable by court marshal and put our entire squadron and those near us at terrible risk. We were unable to see to positively identify the guilty parties, or we would have been able to report them. Flying above us gave them an advantage so they remained undistinguishable.

We completed our mission as ordered and by the grace of God, returned to the base unscathed. We reported this incident to our interrogation officer immediately on our return to the base. He was adamant about finding out who had disobeyed orders and vowed to find and court martial the guilty parties. That was another close one and I thank God for our safe return.

I overheard another crew that was being interrogated at the same time and heard their harrowing experience on that same Singapore mission.

These poor guys experience made ours seem trivial by comparison. They were flying to the IP alone at 8,000 feet, and were hit by a tremendous gust of wind that swept the bomber upwards to 20,000 feet. The plane peaked, then began descending into a nosedive then began to spiral out of control. The bomb bays were fully loaded and I'm sure the crew feared they had met the end. I can not fathom what it must have been like for that poor crew to suddenly nosedive out of control like that. They were pinned due to the force of the decent and were unable to make even the slightest effort to bail out. I guess you hang on watch and pray fighting dizziness and loss of equilibrium. You pray that the pilot has enough fight in him to regain control.

By the grace of God, the pilot and co-pilot never lost their cool and were able to right the plane after this free fall, miraculously saving themselves. Supposedly by making small adjustments on the horizontal trim tabs of the tail, the pilot ended up righting the plane, ultimately regaining control of the craft. The whole crew was so shaken that they aborted the mission and returned to base.

The pilot and crew reported that they were swept up like a feather in the wind with virtually no control. After landing and reporting the mishap to the interrogation officers, they were grounded for three months due to their near death experience.

Singapore, being close to the equator, was also subject to extremely erratic air stream phenomenon, just as if not worse than were experienced flying of the Hump. In viewing first hand their fear, we knew that God had to be with them.

Chapter XVII

Mission:
Bombing Raid, Burma, Rangoon

On March 17th we were assigned a mission to raid Rangoon, the capital city of Burma that also had been in enemy hands since the attack on Pearl. We carried 56-260 pound cluster bombs and carefully deposited them on an enemy storage depot. We dropped and returned without incident. This mission was an easy one as we met no opposition and were back to the base in 7 hours. On this mission I flew as the Tail Gunner because our regular crew member took ill. I thought it would be a welcome change and I was qualified to do so. The visual perspective from that vantage was wonderful but the isolation made me uncomfortable. I felt that my butt was out there alone, and even though I had that big cannon to protect myself, I didn't like it. That would be the last time I would mount that station and position.

_____

Chapter XVIII

Mission: Mining Saigon

On March 27th we were given a mission to mine the port city of Saigon, French Indo China, better known today as Viet Nam. Camranh Bay was our targeted area because the enemy had been shipping supplies through these corridors so in an effort to disrupt the enemies supply lines mining was used. This was again a long and grueling flight however we again met no serious opposition. We carried eight 1,000- pound mines that we strategically placed quickly and effortlessly and then made our turn and headed back to the base.

Just as our last mining mission, the tail gunner reported seeing activity as the Japanese scurried to man the antiaircraft guns.

"We woke them up again" the tail gunner says over the inter-com.

"Slightly after the fact," I replied as we were long gone, out of their range.

"Too little, too late, for the people of the rising sun" Shep interjects.

Our mission had been successfully accomplishment, and executed without flaw. We had flown in under enemy radar at an altitude of 4,000 feet, and had gotten in and out unchallenged. This type of mission was good for our egos.

We made a few test hops during the first weeks of April but soon heard rumors that we would be following the other units that were being relocated.

"So what do you think, you going to miss this place Tex" I question.

"Oh yea, like a hound dog misses scratching fleas" he replies,

Most other groups had begun to evacuate India for the newly captured Islands of Mariana's group throughout the early part of March, so our remaining time was spent in preparation of the move.

While some groups flew their combat weary bombers to the island group, we were taken by ship to our new home, and this trip was long.

Map of Area

Chapter XIX

Trip to Tinian

In April we were issued orders to leave India towards the end of the month. Our entire group was taken via Army transport trucks to Calcutta where we boarded a troop ship. The Navy issued us life preservers, and we were told to wear them 24 hours a day while on the ship. On April 30, 1945 we set sail and faced the drudgery of life at sea. Our bunks were located in the hull, about 6 stories down in the deep, dank recesses of the ship. Air was so stagnant down there, and it was so claustrophobic that I didn't want to stay there for a minute, let alone sleep there. Many of us found more comfortable sleeping arrangements on the deck of the ship, so while the weather permitted we did so.

We were given strict orders about smoking while aboard ship. While permitted during the day it was strictly prohibited at night, and we were told that anyone who disobeyed the no smoking rule would be put in the brig. We all knew the obvious reason and followed the rules. After a week of travel we stopped in Perth, Australia for supplies and fuel.

We stayed in Perth for two days and while we ate and slept on the ship, we were able to go ashore to sightsee or whatever. The majority of the group went looking for a bar or the other places that might help relieve the stresses of young lonely men. I walked around town just looking around, and found the Australians to be very friendly and eager to chat and hear news of the war. Perth was not modern by any stretch of the imagination. Most buildings were old, there was no indoor plumbing but after all we were used to that by then. The local people were great and this was a wonderful change of pace and scenery.

We headed North upon leaving Australia and were in route to the Mariana's Island group in the Pacific. For the most part of the days during the trip the GI's would stay on deck, until these torrential rains began. At that time we returned to our bunks and tried to tolerate life in the recesses of the ship. There were high seas during the storms and many GI's became ill from motion sickness. The closeness and stagnant air in the bunks were also contributors. It rained for a few days and time seemed to stand still as we would occasionally go on the deck to break the monotony. The strangest phenomenon was when we finally broke from the rain. This black cloud that had followed us for days suddenly ended and within seconds the sun is shining like we were back in Miami Beach. I guess we out ran the storm and not having any reference point distorts both time and space. Just miles upon miles of rolling seas disoriented me. I was glad that I was in the Air Force.

When we passed the equator there was some kind of celebration aboard the ship. It seems that the crew of the troop ship would dunk some of the airmen in celebration of the crossing. I never quite figured out what that was all about. But, as the saying goes, While in Rome, so we enjoyed the festivities. We were passengers on their ship and this was like a fraternal type of hazing. I guess they wanted to initiate the fly boys, as there was always rivalry between the different branches of the service. It was all done in good taste and we all laughed.

Our next stop and final destination was the Mariana's Group in the Pacific Ocean. We anchored on May 25th, 1945 a half mile off shore of Tinian. The newly constructed channel was not deep enough to accommodate the ship, so we would have to be ferried by smaller boats to the island.

After nearly a month on that troop ship, with our personal gear loaded on our backs, we made preparations to disembark. We were instructed to climb down the rope ladders over the side of the ship to waiting motor boats. I don't think these were ladders; they looked more like cargo nets. They were about 40 feet wide and 10 at a time we descended downward. I weighted in at a strapping 113 pounds at the time and my full gear and helmet weighed nearly as much as I did. With this amount of weight on my back and the swaying of the ship, my sense of balance was off during the decent. Further complicating things amidst this chaos, the Navy personal barked orders to us, "Keep going, don't look down" through megaphones. As we inched downward I did look down once, and seeing this little boat bobbing like a cork in the ocean, and the distance I yet had to travel I stopped….. frozen with fear. The guy above me coming down nearly used my head as a ladder rung so this instantly nudged me back into movement.

"Sorry Mack he said, as he almost loses his grip

"Yea Yea" I reply immediately regaining momentum.

When I reached the bottom there were Navy personal there assisting us into the small craft. They ferried us to our new home.

The Northern Mariana Islands are made of a three island group; Guam, Tinian, and Saipan. Tinian had been occupied by Japan as a pursuit of Colonial Expansionism after World War One.

Germany had lost all control of its possessions including the Northern Mariana Islands after being defeated and left bankrupt. Guam was purchased by the United States while Saipan and Tinian were purchased by the Japanese for use in Colonial Expansionism.

Japanese proposed use of the islands was primarily agricultural, and while the rest of the world was somewhat skeptical, the League of Nations ultimately gave Japan control of these islands. This was under severe opposition from America, and with strict regulations, and the stipulations that there was to be no military development, Japan readily agreed and took and maintained control of these two islands.

Over the years, Tinian was developed as just that, an agricultural island. It supplied Japan's appetite for sugar. It was an island that had long been occupied by a native population, and had assimilated into the Japanese culture. As time progressed, Japan's quest for expansionism and the islands strategic and military value lead to its fortification under a shroud of secrecy. As Japan prepared for war, they created military installations, landing strips, built fortified bomb shelters and placed strategic armament throughout the islands.

Prior to the American invasion, the island had been pounded for weeks with heavy naval bombardment, and in a fierce battle our marines and our GI's stormed the beaches of Tinian. That was three months earlier and our forces had successfully secured the island for the United States. This was done with strategic military precision as Japan had been expecting a large scale American invasion.

The Japanese Empire fortified every possible venue capable of supporting such a large scale assault of the island, or so they thought. In an assessment of intelligence, it was deemed that 2 small beaches would ultimately be the launch site of the invasion. Never in history had such a feat been attempted as the beaches were so small they had been dismissed by the Japanese military strategist as being of no significant importance. These were tiny and unimportant and therefore were not heavily defended.

Big mistake for The Empire, as they lost thousands of men and control of the island during the take over. Even though there was such a heavy onslaught of Naval bombardment prior to the invasion, many of these fortifications were largely still intact, a credit to the ingenuity and resourcefulness of the enemy. The enemy suffered greatly as firefights were the principle means of extricating them from hiding.

The Mariana Group in the Pacific had been taken from the Japanese and was transformed to a base capable of landing the B-29. This would be the new home for our bombers and its location was of strategic value for the onslaught that would soon be unleashed on Japan.

Our Sea-Bee's had been called in to construct runways, barracks, mess halls, and headquarters on this beautiful island. They constructed these facilities in record time to wage the war on the Japanese mainland, working twenty four hour shifts, seven days a week. Resourceful in their efforts, they created huge runways needed for the B-29's from the processed coral on the island.

There was a magazine called Yank printed for the western Pacific that had stories and information of the CBI Theatre and included pictures of the GI's, and what was happening with the war in the Pacific. Upon our arrival, the magazine featured the newly acquired Mariana Island group, and the caption underneath the picture stated; Wait Till The 58th Gets Here.

. Apparently we had a reputation, and they expected great things from us, being that we were all seasoned combat crews.

We settled into this beautiful island of white coral. The coral was so white, clean and bright that you had to squint to see. It was so white and bright that you couldn't't see that well and you experience a form of snow blindness from the intensity of brightness. In an effort to protect our eyes, the Air Force issued us protective sunglasses to shade the brightness. This island seemed such an idyllic place to be, so beautiful and was a far cry from what we had left in India.

While adjusting to our new surroundings and acquainting ourselves with the island, we wandered to the southern most point of the island's beach.

"Now this is more like it" I said to the group

"Wonder how the chow is here" was another question that we asked.

"Anything's an improvement" I blurted out.

Apparently things were much better here than the Hell Hole we had been living in. This was totally different than I had ever seen before, the south Pacific seemed like paradise

"Lets' go check out the beach, and go for a swim" came a suggestion, and the major consensus was in agreement. We walked quite a distance and finally arrived at the swimming beach, and as we entered the water on the rugged rocky coral beach, these small beautifully colored tropical fish darted to and fro from rock to rock just under our feet.

"Look at these fish" I pointed out to Shep. "Gentleman, this is a far cry from Atlantic City."

"Hey watch they don't bite you, they might give you a case of the Japanese Crud or something. I read somewhere that there are some fish that are poisonous" says Gunther, our new tail gunner.

"Read, when did you learn how to read" I said jokingly.

They had the most brilliant and beautiful colors I had ever seen. Blues, deeper than the bluest skies, and vibrant oranges and intensely blinding yellows. Magnificent to the point that I could watch them for hours if this were another place and time. But the reality was, there were still Japanese soldiers that had evaded capture hiding in the caves on the island, and we were forewarned. So anytime we visited the beach, there were always a few of us standing guard looking for the enemy. We were always conscious of that fact and we never let our guard down. We always carried our shoulder holsters with our 45's to defend ourselves if necessary.

It was quite a trek to the beach being that we were housed in Quonset huts on the West side of the island near the four 10,000 foot runways that had been constructed. We did take advantage on every possible occasion to visit the beach between missions, and I do recall on one of the trips there, we had been relaxing when out in the distance I saw a large dark funnel cloud forming. It was a dark, black, swirling mass stretching from the ocean floor to what seemed to be a thousand feet in the sky. I think they are now called "waterspouts" and now I'm not from Kansas, I hadn't yet seen The Wizard of Oz' yet, and I'll admit that I might have been a bit naive, but I DID know that this looked like some sort of tornado and it appeared to be coming our way. We all ran back to the safety of our barracks as fast as possible in anticipation of the major storm about to strike. We waited and waited but it never came.

Did we ever take a ribbing from our colleagues about the storm! I guess it turned and went out to sea or whatever those things do. Go figure. Those releases from the reality were fleeting but welcome as we were about to turn up the heat on Japan.

Tinian was now the home of the largest concentration of B-29's in the Pacific, with numbers in the 700 plus range and there were always an additional fifty planes or so being repaired at any given time. As a result, takeoffs were staggered at 50 second increments to accommodate the vast numbers that were taking off for missions. It was such a wonderful sight to see these planes taking off as the sky filled with these beautiful bombers.

There were four 10,000 foot runways at West Field, on the island, and they would take off in sync from each of the four runways. It was always an exercise in precision and for an hour and a half the sky would be illuminated with these silver bombers.

An added plus to being in Tinian was that my good friends Nino, and Salvatore were both stationed there. I had no idea that they were here, until one day out of the blue, both these guys come into our barracks asking "where's the skinny Greek Kid from New Jersey."

Boy, those two were a sight for sore eyes.

Ready For Take Off

_____

Chapter XX

Mission:
Raid on Tomoiko, Japan

Our first mission from Tinian over The Empire took place on June 10th, 1945. It was a daylight mission that we would fly to the target without fighter escort, and then rendezvous at the IP before the bomb run. We carried twenty-two 500 pound general purpose bombs, and our target was the Japan Aircraft Co in Tomoiko, Japan. The flight took us 7 hours to reach the target area. We were part of a group of 32 bombers sent to destroy this target. During this mission is where we got our first taste of the new weapon Japan had in store for us, the infamous "Kamikaze." A swarm of Mitsubishi Zeros attacked our formation as we were entering the slot into formation. One of our planes was hit and I witnessed the flash of impact as it began its descent and then plummet downward from the sky. One consolation was that I did see the crew bail out and some chutes open far down below us. Two fighters approach us, and I had a square bead on these little bastards. They came in at three o'clock high, my side. I had seen them coming in and had them set up, and as they came into range I lit into the first. Without saying a word or even having time to think I tagged him with a broadside fire. With my fingers glued to the trigger the first bursts of our fifties lit into them. I stayed locked on target as the guns sent out a barrage of lead towards him. Tracers flying past him, I stayed focused on him and then I tagged him as I saw the plane flame as the wing tanks explode and he began to spiral, nose-diving like a corkscrew earthbound. I still stayed on him, or as best as I could, I wanted to make sure he couldn't't maneuver into one of our aircraft.

The second enemy fighter had chosen another plane in our formation to instill his venom, but was also unsuccessful, as he had been tagged and failed to ram either of us. This was a brief encounter that totaled maybe seven seconds but it was an extremely frightful few seconds. That second plane came close enough to us on his uncontrollable decent from the sky to cause us concern, but was unable to complete his mission. We knew they were about to ram us, but all we could do was to hit them as hard and often as possible to prevent that from happening.

Our biggest fear was encountering the Kamikaze. Our briefings had told us of this technique of desperation that the enemy began using, and of measures to elude this type of attack. The lack of regard of their own lives made them a formidable threat. The only way to combat this, was to whack them so brutally that they couldn't maneuver the plane into you. As a result, every time these little bastards tried us, we threw everything we could at them as hard and fast as we could.

These little divine wind fliers (the literal Japanese translation) thought dying for their emperor is the honorable thing to do, I show you the honorable thing to do you little bastards as I pumped as much lead into them as fast as I could. It was scary and took all the courage you could muster but it had to be done. Our philosophy was, it's either us or them. So, we hammered them, and did so relentlessly.

We got in and dropped our bomb load on the aircraft manufacturing company, and made it home safely, never seeing another enemy aircraft on this trip.

Our presence was surely intimidating to the enemy as we gained air superiority. They were out gunned, outnumbered, and knew only too well that the noose was tightening around The Empire's' neck. That is the most difficult time for the enemy and the most dangerous defensively as they move towards desperation for the cause.

I always carried that small sledge hammer at my station, and positioned it within reach, right next to my blister window on all missions. I purchased the tool while in Calcutta, after hearing stories about trapped gunners, and wanted to be prepared in the event that we were ever hit. As a waist gunner I had read that the Plexiglas blisters that were on each side of the plane were susceptible to blow-outs under stress in the early planes, and although the problem had been supposedly rectified, maybe it had been rectified too well. I still needed a little assurance.

One instance in particular was that of a side gunner that had seen the potential danger to his life during such a blow-out, and made a harness that would keep him safely inside the plane in the event of such a disaster. Using discarded parachute harnesses he designed a system that allowed enough slack for him to function unencumbered while performing his duties on the plane, but yet was secure enough to keep him tethered inside the plane if such and accident were to occur. Whether by fate or premonition, his greatest fear was realized as his blister did blow out on a mission. The plane was pressurized flying at a higher elevation and as a result of the blow-out and the subsequent de-pressurization of the plane, the unthinkable happened. The gunner was actually sucked out of the plane fuselage. The crew ran to his aid and successfully pulled him back into the plane after about 10 minutes of a very creative rescue. I think the extent of his injuries was frostbite from exposure, but he made a full recovery. He had been knocked unconscious and had been jostled around while dangling from the plane, but due to the perseverance of the crew, they saved him.

Planes that were flying in his formation were actually able to photograph the harrowing ordeal and I saw the pictures back at our base. I still have a picture that I obtained showing this poor fellows plight. So needless to say, the blister windows were re-designed to prevent reoccurrence of this type of tragedy. Anyway even with fortification they supposedly still could be broken out in the event of an emergency.

B-29 Blowout

"If I get trapped within the plane and am unable to make it to one of the other emergency exits I'm going to hammer the blister window, and get the hell out of the plane" I told Shep.

"I'll be right behind you" said Shep

I knew full well that it would depressurize the plane and hopefully I could make my exit from this point. I knew it was possible to survive such an exit and I was determined to get out of there alive. So I had planned escape routes for each scenario, and with God's help I would make it.

"Hey Nick, what are you building with that hammer," Gunther would constantly ask.

"My ticket out of here" I would reply, "sometimes used to keep unruly tail gunners in line."

It was my security blanket, and while some thought it strange, I really didn't care what they thought. I would carry this little bit of insurance with me throughout the war.

We had a saying that was to become our crew's credo that we had painted on our plane; Home Alive in 45,............. Hell or Heaven in 47". The logic behind this saying was that the Air Force would try to defeat this enemy exclusively by use of strategic air strikes. This was unheard of in those days, and all other branches of US military viewed the Air Force as a secondary means, never primary in defeating an enemy. Historically warfare had never been conducted in this manner, but with the development and implementation of the B-29 as a long range heavy bomber, hopefully would change all that, and spare the need of a traditional type of invasion on Japan.

It was estimated that the casualties of such a land assault would exceed the one million mark, and the time estimated to complete such an endeavor would most likely prolong the war an additional 2 years. That was the logic in the Hell or Heaven in 47 aspect of the saying.

If the Air Force was able to succeed in conquering this enemy, this would not only save many Allied lives, but also change the way future wars would be fought. Hopefully, this would be the war to end all wars and we believed in our cause. We wanted to end this quickly and return home to America, to our loved ones, and our way of lives. We hoped to do it ALIVE in 45, and this credo was indelibly etched in my mind. I wasn't prepared to go down without a fight, I had this basic instinct to survive, and no matter how tough things got I would try to make it.

I had heard of the horrific treatment American flyers faced by the Japanese in capture. The torture, starvation and constant beatings. I didn't have all the answers to the survival puzzle but I would take one thing at a time. I would defend our plane with all the fortitude I had to save us from being downed, but would also be prepared for an escape if necessary. This plan always seemed to have a calming effect on me.

On June 12th we flew a test hop from Tinian, lasting only a few hours. We landed, had our meetings, and attended some ground school classes.

Sometime in March of 1944 our GI's and Marines captured Iwo Jima. This island that is located half way between Japan and Tinian was now being used as a safe haven for planes. During an emergency, we now had a place that was under American command to safely tend to our needs. Whether running low on fuel or being so battered during combat that they were unable to make it home, it was a relief in knowing that we were close enough to be rescued even during the worst scenarios.

Our bomber was forced to use these facilities about six times during missions that we got into trouble. On one such emergency visit, our plane needed repairs, so we had an opportunity to tour the island, seeing the fortified bunkers that the Japanese had constructed during their occupancy. They had constructed the walls with re-enforced concrete that was three to four feet thick.

During the conflict for control, our Navy had bombarded these bunkers with missiles, yet had never really destroyed them. There were large chunks of concrete torn from the bunkers but no shell had ever really penetrated into the bunkers themselves. The GI's, Marines, had to firebomb the enemy from these bunkers with great casualties and loss of life for this strategic island. Luckily, we triumphed, but at a tremendous cost.

Bunkers in Iwo

We followed the same protocol for pre-mission procedures on both India and Tinian. On a daylight mission we would get up early while it was still dark and attend a briefing session. The commanders would tell us how many zeros were in the vicinity how many radar guns they had and also how big and powerful they were. They would name both the primary and secondary target informing us at which altitude we should achieve as we flew over each target and at what initial point (IP) the aircraft were to converge.

We would circle the initial point until we all got into the proper slots of the formation, which would usually be from twenty-five to fifty miles from the target. Only then we would be ready to begin the bombing run. The briefing commanders would tell us the location of the two or three submarines in the vicinity of our return path. In the event that we were to shot up to make it back to the base and were forced to ditch in the Pacific, they would retrieve us. All the crew members stood up to make sure they understood the location of these subs.

We all felt some reassurance upon hearing this information, knowing that the U.S. Government was doing everything in its power to secure the welfare of its flyers. The briefings would last from thirty to forty-five minutes; we would then be dismissed to the mess hall for breakfast. By that time, most of us would be so nervous that who could eat? A few cigarettes and some coffee and then we were taken by truck to West Field to our plane.

The first job for the crew was to spin the propellers on each engine to lubricate the pistons prior to boarding. This lubricated the engine and also insured that there was no hydraulic lock of our operational systems. Upon completion we entered the craft with our parachutes, 45 caliber shoulder holsters, carrying our flak protectors (that covered our backs and chests) and steel helmets.

We would wait until the Initial Point of the bombing run to put on our flak suits and helmets. These offered protection from the flak that was being fired upon us from the antiaircraft units. Once in the plane, the pilot would start the engines and the engineer would go through his checklist. Our engineer was so thorough in his analysis of our vessels status, that the mission would be aborted if anything did not check-out correctly. When everything checked out he would contact the pilot and the pilot in turn would contact the flight tower to get the OK for takeoff. Then we would taxi to the runway in position and wait for our signal from the tower.

Once given the signal, the pilot would rev up the four engines to the proper RPM while keeping the wheels locked by braking. At the proper time the pilot would release the brakes and the plane would lunge forward and we would proceed down the runway gaining speed until we were airborne. This procedure was deemed to provide the optimum way to attain the thrust needed for takeoff considering the tremendous weight of the craft. The majority of the 10,000 foot runway was utilized before the bloated bomber became airborne.

The Norden Bomb Sight we used was one of the best kept secrets of the war. These amazing devises were equipped with gyroscopes, compasses and had the capacity to determine wind speed, air speed, and all other variables; to land our bombs on the target. The bombardier in conjunction with Norden had total control of the plane while flying over the target. The Auto Pilot mode would allow the Norden to calculate trajectory with complete accuracy. These devices were so *Top* Secret that you were ordered to destroy them before letting them get into enemy hands.

92

On bombing runs, the bombardier took control of the plane. The bombardier worked to align the target in the Norden Bomb Sights. Once locked onto the target and after releasing our bomb load the pilot would again regain control of the aircraft then head for the open ocean and proceed home by ourselves.

Once back at the base, trucks would pick up the whole crew and take us to be interrogated answering questions and reporting all information. In the interim we would be given a quart of liquor to share with the eleven members of our crew. Each crew member would take a swig, mostly right out of the bottle, and pass it to the next person. This was the government's way to relax our nerves so we could get some rest. Sometimes the bottle went around three times before everyone was calm enough.

We would follow the same procedures on night missions, reach our coordinates and drop our bomb load. The best part of all missions was immediately after the *Bombs Away* call, and making it to the ocean with no mishaps. During the flight home, I would relax and eat some K Rations to steady my nerves and light up a cigarette. That cigarette did wonders in relieving the stress. I began smoking heavily during that period over Japan, a habit that I quit after the war.

Returning to the base from most night missions, the sun would have come up, beautifully shining and reflecting off the beautiful white clouds that filled the sky. Everything would look so peaceful and serene that it seemed like heaven on earth, and I so looked forward to this part of every mission. One would never know that a terrible war was raging on the ground below.

Chapter XXI

Mission:
Fire Raid on Osaka, Japan

One June 15,1945 at a briefing before a night mission to Osaka, Japan we were told that the target had a large concentration of zeros and powerful radar guns. We would participate by carrying incendiary cluster bombs that were designed to deploy at an altitude of 5,000 feet, and rain fire on the city. Again the briefing officers reiterated that there would be large amounts of defense, and that this would be a massive undertaking with many bomb groups participating in this raid.

I guess that mission after mission begins to take its toll on your nerves, and whether it was psychological or not one of my teeth began to ache. It began to throb, right after the briefing so I went to the dentist to have it checked out. I had plenty of time before our plane was to depart for the mission.

The dentist had a drilling machine that he operated with his foot, like a treadle sewing machine. He drilled the cavity and gave me a temporary filling.

"Doc, this is killing me" I said to the dentist as he completed his filling.

"It's bad hugh" I mumbled, my speech distorted by the fingers and other apparatus in my mouth.

"We'll take care of everything" replies the dentist.

"So, what group are you with?"

"Ifty eith" I reply I can't even understand myself I thought to myself, Why's this guy conversing with me when I've got this much stuff in my mouth.

When he was finished I asked him if he thought it would be fine for me to go on the scheduled mission that evening, hoping that my condition warranted a reprieve.

"You'll be perfectly fine" he said reassuringly. "You've got nice teeth"

Nice teeth I said to myself, who cares about nice teeth,

"I'm in a lot of pain."

He reassured me I would be fine, and sent me on my way.

I went on the mission with my fears controlling me and after a while I calmed myself down and the nervousness subsided. I convinced myself that if it were my time there was nothing I could do about it.

We flew to Osaka in less than perfect weather and had been given fighter escort for the first time ever. P51's had flown with us for a while, but turned back due to inclement weather. They also had a much more limited range capability, so they said their adieu, and we were on our own. Seems like some things never change.

We reached the IP and made our way into the bombing formation slot. As we progressed toward the target area we begin to encounter light enemy flak. The cloud cover contributed to the inaccuracy of Anti-aircraft fire, and it did not appear to be a threat. One good thing about flak is that if it's being thrown at you, no enemy fighters are in the area.

The bombardier controls the plane, and again appears to be taking to much time.

"What's going on", I ask Tex, "can you see anything?"

As the words leave my mouth he releases the incendiaries, the plane lurches upwards as the bombs away signal squawks from the inter-com and we turn to exit the area.

Flak immediately started exploding around us in that awful ack-ack sound that we all learned to associate with danger. The interior of the plane is lit up so brightly that it seems like daylight. That's one of the most intimidating feelings I have ever experienced. The darkness of night is seductive in its ability to provide secrecy, security and stealth. Now we were observed, violated, the hunter had become the hunted. The plane shook from the resonating explosion as it jarred us with such intensity that it resonated within my tooth. Needless to say, I didn't think of my tooth for long. There was no time to think of anything else but to get out of this situation. There was this new product that we were introduced to a few weeks ago that supposedly had the capacity to jam the enemies radar. We had been given a case of this product, and hadn't had the opportunity to use it. Looks like today was the day.

We were all at our stations as I move to the isolated camera hatch and began hurling spools of *Window*, sometimes referred to as *Radar Rope* out of the opening. As it began to unfurl, the enemy radar started tracking the trail of aluminum downwards, away from us, and with that, those powerful lights followed and once again we were in the security of semi darkness. The pilot changed elevation and we were safe again.

"Hey, that stuff is pretty good" Shep comments as I return to my station.

"Yea it sure got us out of a jam" I reply

"Oh, how's your tooth" Shep questions

"What tooth" I reply.

Eight hours later, we returned to our base in Tinian, glad to have made it home. We did experience some flak damage to the plane but nothing major.

We reported the situation at our debriefing, and commented that the *Window* had been a lifesaver on the mission and, from what I gather it's still used today, although it is now pulverized and called *Chaff.*

Never once did it occur to me to quit or abandon flying. I don't know why. I guess I was raised not to be a quitter, or it might have been that I never thought of it. We all knew we were tough and were fighting for our country. Never the less our effectiveness on the Japanese Air

95

Force was devastating. We were now hitting them on a daily basis and restricting their ability to get supplies with the mining of their harbors. We were clearly the dominant force, and this air superiority was greatly diminishing the enemy's numbers and effectiveness. Both in the sky, and on the seas, the effectiveness of our bombing raids was evident. It is with this premise that the B-29 was designed, and it had risen to the challenge delivering devastating effectiveness on the enemy.

Chapter XXII

Mission:
Fire Raid on Omuta, Japan

On June 18th we participated in an incendiary attack on the urban city of Omuta. We were part of a force of 116 bombers that attacked the city. We had 184 small 100 pound fire bombs that were to explode a few thousand feet above the city and destroy it. We blanketed the city with fire as these incendiaries ravaged everything below and while seeing some enemy aircraft, none of them engaged us in any capacity. This mission took 16 hours to complete.

Chapter XXIII

_____

Mission:
Fire Raid on Toyohashi, Japan

On June 20th our target was Toyohashi, Japan. We had forty 500 pound incendiary (fire) bombs, twenty in each bomb bay. There were large numbers of bombers participating in this raid; as a result we were lined up waiting for our turn for takeoff.

We were delayed on the runway, for what seems to be a long time, oblivious to any problem, when we receive notice to divert to another runway.

Apparently there was the wreckage of a bomber that had burst into flames before becoming airborne blocking the runway on Westfield, and it was closed due to the catastrophe. This had happened before, and we all knew the drill, so after a brief delay, some maneuvering, and repositioning we approached the runway, and began our take-off.

Upon becoming air-borne, while looking out my blister window, I saw evidence of the disaster, with smoke and debris littering the last quarter of the runway of Westfield. Just by the debris field, I knew that no-one would have been able to survive that type of disaster.

"Those poor guys didn't have a chance" I thought to myself, as our bomber gains altitude,

"Flaps retracting, landing gear retracted" I report to the pilot, preoccupied with my duties and thoughts of the impending mission.

We flew over the target that night at an altitude of only 5,000 feet. This mission differed from others in the sense that there was no group formation; therefore every Bomber hit the target alone. There was thick black smoke from the hundreds of planes that had previously dropped their bombs. It was surely hell on earth as our planes rained fire on the target. The black pitch of the Thermal Cloud raised at least 30,000 feet high and it totally engulfed us as I attempted to look from my blister window. The smell was nauseating; I thought it was that of burning flesh. The heat was unbearable, as all the wooden constructed buildings below fueled this inferno.

We were on automatic pilot (standard procedure over the target) as the bombardier read the coordinates, and made adjustments. Thank you to that basic mechanical computer technology of the Norden Bomb Sights, because the plane would have been almost impossible to handle manually. I'll always remember the turbulence and the ferociousness of the smoke and fire below, the incredible heat and that putrid stench.

Even though we all were somewhat de-sensitize to the death and destruction around us, being subjected to that smell brought the reality of what we were doing into my psyche.

I couldn't help thinking of the humanity suffering, as visions of people ablaze ran through my head. My next thought is the exploded bomber from this morning on West Field, and the horror of those poor guys, as a wave of fear, and anxiety envelops me.

"Start thinking right" I say to myself out loud, "get those thoughts out of your head, you're going to make it..... calm down now" as the thoughts begin to diminish.

"Man, I'm glad were out of there" says Shep

"Whew, me too" I reply, "That stench, it's unbearable"

We made our way home as I fought the urge to be sick, while maintaining a watch for the enemy, and was relieved when we landed back at the base.

We made our way to the debriefing room, and I grabbed the traditional comfort in a bottle, and took a major swig, then another, until I felt the alcohol instill calmness throughout my body.

Walking out of the room to the outside, I see Salvatore sitting down, his face covered by his hands. As I approach him and call his name, he slowly lifts his head, his eyes swollen, and face distorted, as he wipes the tears from his eyes,

"It's Nino" he says, his face flooding with tears.

"No, No, No.......... how" I question, as my eyes begin to well up.

"It was his plane..... This morning.......on the runway" replies Sal.

We both sat there, grief stricken, silent for some time, as I recalled the horror from the mission, knowing that Nino's plane was also full of incendiaries, and that they had exploded on the runway.

"Nino was a great guy, a true friend and will be sorely missed" I say, as Sal and I try and console each other.

The military teaches you how to become men, about honor in serving your country, but never about dealing with emotions.

I went and spoke to the chaplain, and purged myself of some of the emotion and pain, and I'm sure Sal did the same, as we met later on in the day, and had a drink in the memory of our fallen friend.

Chapter XXIV

Mission:
Raid on Kure, Japan

On June 22nd, not two days after the loss of my good friend, we participated in a bombing raid on the Kure Naval Arsenal in Japan. We were part of a large group that was designated to destroy the Arsenal, and were equipped with 8- 1000 pound general purpose bombs in our pay-load. I believe that we were joined by the 73rd bomb wing for this mission, and between the 58th and 73rd there were close to two hundred planes on this mission. This was a dangerous mission, and the arsenal was well fortified and defended. We merged into the formation and let loose our loads on the arsenal. There were many enemy fighters, although none engaged us, and while flak was heavy we managed to hit the target effectively and return without significant damage, although we landed at Iwo Jima for additional fuel. We got back far later than most due to our unscheduled stop in Iwo, and were debriefed, and hit the sack due to exhaustion.

It wasn't till the next morning that I heard about Sal's unit, and their reported mishap on the same Kure mission.

I couldn't't believe my ears when I was told, but I felt more optimistic as the story unfolded. It seemed that after having hit their target, his plane was shot up so badly that it was forced to ditch in the Pacific Ocean. There had been radio transmission and the military had a good idea where they were, and had rescue vessels in route.

Having learned of his fate, I had some hope that the crew quite possibly had survived and was on a life raft.

_____

Chapter XXV

Mission:
Raid on Sumitomo Metal Works
Hit Secondary Target of Opportunity, Kushimoto

As luck would have it, our next day's mission was in the same area that Sal's plane was reported ditching. As we neared the area I kept my eye open looking for an orange life raft. That was the morning of June 26th, and I was diligent in my pursuit, when I spotted an orange mass in the water. My hopes escalated as I thought it might possibly be the raft of some survivor, maybe even Salvatore. I radioed the pilot through the intercom and explained that I saw an orange mass in the ocean below and that it could possibly be some survivors. We were flying at 8,000 feet and then the pilot lowered the plane to 4,000 feet. He circled the area to get a closer look. To our dismay, it turned out that the orange mass was the floating debris field; garbage that had been thrown overboard by a departed naval ship. I was so disappointed because I thought we might have found Salvatore.

As a result of this exploration we had lost valuable time, and we were unable to hit our primary target, the Sumitomo Metal Works factory.

We were now forced to hit the secondary target, or a target of opportunity as it was called. This in itself is not a problem; however one of the downfalls in bombing a target of opportunity is that we would hit it alone. While not particularly bad news, it was slightly unsettling as we would attack this target without the benefit of being part of a large group of bombers. There is strength in numbers, but another benefit is that of obscurity. With the thought of facing the enemy alone and with my friends now lost, my fears escalated and I worried about the prospects. Was my luck running out? Were we in for a shellacking? I hoped and prayed that we didn't get rammed by the Zeros or blasted by the antiaircraft fire. I felt guilty that I would have been the culprit for this misfortune. I was tense as we approached the city of Kushimoto with our payload of only 3 large 4,000 pounders. These were classified as general purpose bombs and we dropped them over the city. My eyes were constantly scanning the area in defense of our plane. Luckily we hit the target, made our turn towards home, and got out of there without mishap.

The trip back was long and both mentally and physically exhausting.

However, I had the fortitude to keep an eye out for life rafts. I found out later that Salvatore's plane and crew were never found.

In reality, the odds of finding someone while flying a mission were next to impossible. The vastness of the Pacific is incomprehensible and we had no nautical charts or vague information of the exact location that the plane went down. There were tidal conditions and a host of other variables that effect the movement of life rafts. We really had no conformation that they even were successful in the ditching, but I felt an obligation to do whatever was in my power to do.

In hindsight I realize that I was looking for the proverbial needle in a haystack but as we all know, hindsight is always 20/20. Under even the most optimum conditions while ditching, the pilot puts the plane into a belly land and even if the ocean is calm there are only a few minutes at most to scramble to the emergency exits. During these chaotic seconds you must find your way out of the wreckage, locate and take whatever survival gear you can get your hands on. Your life jacket (Mae West), rubberized boat, flares, radio, pistol, etc. and hopefully you are not injured during, or prior to the ditching.

Anyway, the loss of these two friends was difficult for me to handle. They had become family and I felt such sorrow for their losses. There is this terrible empty feeling in your gut and you cannot help but reminisce of the good times we all had during the grieving process. That brought back the sorrow and this truly began to affect me. In an effort to overcome this loss, I pulled myself together and made a conscious effort to stay as busy as possible and not allow myself to think about it.

Our survival depended on everyone being, and giving 100% and I was no exception. That rigorous time schedule left me little time to think of my sorrows.

I, still today, remember both my friends; that Sal was from Massachusetts and that he was a really chubby young man. That was kind of a rarity as most people of the depression era were pencil thin. Sal said that during the depression all his family ate was pasta, in one form or another. As a result, his weight had ballooned upwards. He was determined to get back into good shape and worked at calisthenics diligently. He really had slimmed down. He was a full head and then some taller than me. We were all friends, the three of us. We always hung around together, joked with each other, and took trips into town together. As a matter of fact, during most of the fun escapades that I have written about, these guys were there.

"Boys, if you're listening up there, and I know you are, It was a privilege and honor to have served with both of you, and I was blessed having had your friendship, even if only for a brief time". You are not forgotten.

I thanked God for the continued good fortune and I knew that it was my faith that kept me going on mission after mission.

Chapter XXVI

Mission:
Second Raid on Kure

On July 2ⁿᵈ, 1945 we flew a daylight raid mission over the port city Kure, on the main island of Honshu, Japan. Kure had facilities for dry docking their warships and was home to the Hiro Naval Base, among other wartime factories. I don't think our briefing officers knew that there were two Japanese destroyers that were in dry dock for repairs at the time of our second attack. This area had been hit previously and we were sent back to launch another incendiary attack. We were carrying 182-100 pound incendiary bombs and were flying in formation over the target. As the bomb bays opened I looked below and saw the two destroyers being worked on. This being such an industrial city, it was well protected. We dropped our load and descended into a turn to make our escape. We ran smack into a barrage of anti aircraft fire so intense that I was almost knocked off my feet.

We all had our Flak suits on and while very cumbersome, they were designed with the purpose of saving our lives. The two destroyers below, plus the Hiro Naval bases anti aircraft guns opened up on us, pelting us relentlessly as the sound of flak resonate against our plane. The almost gravel sounding effect of spewing shrapnel over the entire length of the plane assured us that their radar guns had locked onto our altitude.

We were in trouble and were in the midst of heavy flak field with nowhere to go. Our plane was sustaining serious damage, and would not withstand much more of this intensity of fire.

It was my task again to jam enemy radar, and the method and procedure for deploying these defenses as I spoke of before, was not technical by any stretch of the imagination. While new and only been given to us a few missions earlier, it had been extremely effective in the past. Being made of the same material as our bombers, these spools would unfurl earthbound in long lengths. As they whirled downwards, the enemy radar guns turned and track them as they fell. By doing so, this essentially jammed their radar which left us free of flak for a short period.

Flak is this dangerous type of explosive shell that is fired into the sky. It explodes at the altitude determined by the radar. The fragments of this projectile penetrate the plane and can cause enough damage to bring a plane down. You would see these bursting around you and view the different color of the explosion. They detonate with an awful ack-ack sound that you learn quickly to associate with danger. There is shrapnel flying in every direction at 8,000 feet, and this flak could hit any number of things, us personally, our bombs, or fuel tanks, with devastating results. It would cause the plane to explode in mid-air.

Back to the mission, the whole crew was aware of our situation, and we were all panicked with urgency. There was terror in the voices of the crew, as their intensity of emotion came through the intercom, we were in serious trouble.

"They've got our mark, jam the radar, get them off of us" is all I heard.

"They've got out mark, Damn it Nick, hurry" The voices were overshadowed by the explosions as I continued to toss the spools of Window radar rope from the hatch. As fast as I could reach for them, sometimes three at a time, I continued, incessantly as the safety and fate of the crew was in my hands. The fury of their tone reflected the urgency of the situation, my field of vision being restricted to the 2X2 openings of the camera hatch but I knew from feeling the plane lurching from the explosions of our predicament. The other crew members had more of a peripheral view and the enemy definitely had a bead on us and our altitude pegged. Caught up in the moment, my heart pounding through this chaos, I tossed unremittingly until we finally succeeded in breaking from the flak field. After what seemed like an eternity I had almost emptied the entire case, but that's what it was there for, and we had broken away.

This was the closest we had ever been to being shot down. My hands shook and I felt the urge to be sick in my stomach. We were all elated to have had made it out and the crew acknowledged me for a job well done. I was so shaken that it took three hours for me to finally calm down. When we landed at our base after a seven hour return trip, I was still jumpy from that near miss of flying 8000 feet over hell.

We were forced to relive the incident while being interrogated. Verbatim, we spoke of every nuance of the mission as our interrogation officers scribbled notes. The crew members patted me on the back again for a job well done. This was one of those missions that required at least four to five swigs of Whiskey to calm our nerves down, and upon completion of the interrogation, I requested another case of window from the gunnery captain. He checked his ledger on a clipboard, he advised me that the case I had should have lasted three missions.

I explained the situation again in detail reliving every subtlety of the mission. I told him that the enemy had our altitude and the flak was so intense it created chaos. The flak was so very close to us, it jostled the plane,

"Sir, with all due respect, they had us, and if I didn't do everything in my power to prevent being shot down, we wouldn't be standing here now."

"Sir in my position how would you have handled it? Hearing again and again they've got us, they have our altitude as the explosions pelt the plane with flak, knowing full well that we were goners unless we broke from the flak field. I was doing all I could to avoid being shot down over enemy positions and ultimately we used the majority of the case, Sir. I was using it for the purpose that it was designed for."

Whether he got the picture or not, I wasn't leaving without another case and it defied my logic for him to try to withhold it. As I stood there looking him straight in the eye he did issue me another case, although with some reluctance.

Chapter XXVII

Mission:
Super Dumbo

On July 4th we flew what was called a Super Dumbo Mission to aid in the recovery of downed crews over enemy areas. We followed the paths that our bombers would be returning, and tried to locate any survivors that we might be able to assist in their recovery. Our altitude was 1000 feet, and we were given specific areas to search, along with supplies of food, water, and large life rafts that we could deploy if we found any of our comrades. We searched diligently and spent a total of 16 + hours searching for downed survivors. Unfortunately, we were not lucky enough to find any downed flyers on the trip. We knew that if it had been us in the life rafts, our brothers would, without question, do the same for us. They would put the same effort to aid in our retrieval.

Mission:
Fire Raid on Chiba

On July 7th we took part in a fire raid on the urban city of Chiba. There were 184-100 pound fire bombs that we unleashed on the city, burning the urban areas causing considerable damage to the city and severe smoke over the target. We saw enemy aircraft and were prepared to engage them however they made no aggressive attack on us whatsoever. There was considerable flak but we came through unscathed, and at one point I grabbed the portable oxygen tank, and put it on to avoid having to experience that awful stench that I associated with death. It worked well, and I thanked Shep for the idea he had given me during the toilet episode. The return trip went without any type of aggression from the enemy. This mission lasted 15 hours.

Mission:
Raids on Sendai, And Urban Utsunomiya

On July 10th we also participated on yet another fire raid, on the city of Sendai. This was another urban area that we pelted with 184-100 pound incendiary bombs. We flew in at 8,000 feet and had a clear view of the city. There was flak and I did see some enemy aircraft in the

105

vicinity but again, there was no action taken to engage us in combat. This mission took 16 hours to complete.

On July 13th we raided the urban Utsunomiya, Japan and rained fire on this city. We launched 184-100 pound incendiaries on the target. We saw a few enemy aircraft but were again unchallenged. There was some flak but we made it home in 16 hours.

As you can see by the dates, we were being called on almost a daily basis to deliver the assault against the enemy. We had been successful with our incendiary attacks in totally destroying whole cities and apparently all our mining effort had significantly reduced the ability of the Japanese to re-supply themselves with the raw materials they needed to continue such a war. Even their failure to attempt to engage us seemed indicative of where this war was going.

There seemed time to get a little relaxation in before our next mission. A few of us got together and decided to spend the day at the beach. There had been no problems of the enemy lurking on the island. They had all been caught and these prisoners were interned in a compound with a tall chain link fence, guarded by the MP's. There were both male and female prisoners although the women were mostly native to the island and had assimilated into the Japanese culture. The men were kept separate and were made to maintain and build roads on the island. They were all well cared for, by the standards of being POW's, much better that their countrymen showed our captive boys.

So as we passed their area of containment, the topic of discussion became the self defense training that we had received versus the training we thought the Japanese had received. My opinion was that anyone with boxing experience should be able to hold his own against the Japanese who were trained in Judo. I knew about boxing and stood behind my belief and statement. We talked about, and rehashed the topic for a good ten minutes, and just as we neared the beach don't you just know it, we happened on a group of these detainees doing road work. A crew member put out a challenge to me. He picked the largest Jap there and motioned to him that I wanted to fight him. The Jap had no idea what was going on and didn't want any trouble. After all he was getting three squares a day, and that was a whole lot better than he had gotten while serving Japan. The group wanted to wager on the outcome of boxing versus Judo. This kind of put me in a bad way and somewhat of an underdog because this Jap weighted at least 50 pounds more than I did.

Now I had gotten myself into a pickle, and if I backed down I would never hear the end of it, so I motioned to him that I wanted to box with him. He looked at me not knowing what was going on, and his reluctance was all I needed. I turned and walked away, back towards the beach, and while I had just saved face I thought to myself, thank God that guy didn't accept the challenge, as I think I might have been out classed.

Chapter XXVIII

Mission:
Fire Bomb Numazu

On July 17th it was the city of Numazu where we participated in a group of approximately 120 aircraft that fire-raided the city. These missions had become almost routine, or as routine as humanly possible. There were some fighters that came up, but they were only a handful, and never aggressively engaged us. We were in twelve plane formations over the target, and unleashed our 184 -100 pounders all fused to explode at 5,000 feet above the city. There was such smoke and turbulence as the city beneath us was totally engulfed in this wrath from hell. This rain of fire would destroy all remnants of what this city ever was before that July day. As we banked a turn after the salvo to head for home we experienced some flak, and reported some light damage to our plane. One of our engines begins to emit a long dark swathe of smoke, and is immediately shut down, and the prop feathered. This shouldn't be any cause for concern at this time of the mission as we continue on our way homebound. We had flown back from missions before with an engine down, so the situation seemed not to be serious at the time. We were heading for home, and that was fine by me, but there was still an additional seven hours before we could call this mission done.

While relaxing somewhat, although still searching for any enemy aircraft, I began thinking about what we were doing, and how the effects of our fire-bombing were winning the war. What I couldn't understand is why the enemy wouldn't surrender, and how much longer they would hold on.

I looked back and was able to view the remnants of the devastation we had just caused. The sky had turned dark gray in color, filled with smoke, and intense fires burning out of control for what seemed to be miles and miles.

"There was life there until an hour ago," I thought to myself. How could anyone survive in that inferno, and for the first time, I felt sorrow for the countless lives that had just been lost. This was the first time that I would think of this enemy as people, or thought of the effects of the wrath that we had just delivered. We had demonized them since their attack on Pearl Harbor, and I had witnessed their evil first hand. I saw enemy fighters shooting our men as they attempted to parachute from burning bombers. This is something that you never forget, and leads you to become as barbaric as your enemy.

We enjoyed a peaceful hour or two, when you can relax, have some coffee, or whatever food is available, and as I gazed out the blister I saw a trail of dark smoke coming from one of our engines. I reported to the pilot, via the intercom, and saw them shut down the engine and feather the prop. We were still about 15 minutes or so from Iwo, and were now in a more serious condition resulting from that Japanese flak field we had flown over. I guess an oil line had ruptured, and again while not in extreme danger we would attempt to make Iwo and land on our two remaining engines. I was just thankful that these engine problems occurred after we dropped our load, and with our plane being 10 tons lighter, our chances of making it were good. Had we sustained this type of damage prior to bombs away, we would be goners.

Our approach was fine as we made all necessary preparations for landing our disabled bomber on the airstrip, and had been given first priority due to our situation. Our landing was picture perfect as we taxied to a hard stand and exited the plane. It was good to be on the ground again, and thank God for Iwo Jima and their facilities. We were debriefed, and spent the evening on Iwo waiting for our engines to be repaired, which due to their need to be replaced turned into a two day stay.

When we returned back to Tinian, we had some down time, and the next mission involved a small test hop, that involved an hour and a half of flight time. That was on July 22, and the rest of the days were spent relaxing or having a few beers with the guys at the PX.

During this time, the women prisoners that were interned seemed to get more and more attractive. I guess the longer we stayed and the drunker we became the better looking they got. There was always someone that talked about trying to get into that area after having consumed a six pack of beer, and that he was going to try his luck that night. This one guy was so focused on how it could be done that he put together a plan on how to accomplish it. In his drunken state he had visions of scaling the fence, bypassing the armed guards, and then having his way with any one of the young ladies that were there. We all laughed at his enthusiasm, and someone asked him if he thought the women would "give it up to him that easily," and he said "why not"……. that he had heard that some officers were privileged to this type of treatment and the poor enlisted men were not.

I don't think it ever happened but it was hilarious to see one of the guys get that fired up. The truth was that most of these ladies were all middle aged or older and were constantly guarded by Military Police. Had this joker ever gotten drunk enough to attempt such a feat, and been lucky enough to have completed it, I would love to have seen his face the morning after, waking up next to an old beater that looked so beautiful the night before. That's when you know that you had too much to drink the night before. It seems that things never change, boys will be boys and these little escapes from the reality made our jobs a tad more bearable.

Chapter XXIX

Mission:
Raid on Osaka, Japan

On July 24th, Osaka was the flavor of the day. Our mission was to destroy the Sumitomo Metal Factory that had produced propellers for enemy aircraft. We were loaded with 6-1,000 pound general purpose bombs and every one of them landed directly on the target. There was severe enemy antiaircraft fire and we did suffer some flak damage. The area affected was close to my station and I saw the extent of damage first hand. I was lucky and as always was wearing my flak suit throughout the combat portion of the mission. After returning from the 16 hour mission, another crew member pointed out to me that I had a large piece of flak lodged into my parachute. Sure enough, a piece of flak had either been deflected by my suit or by the grace of God had lodged itself into my chute. The area that would have been wounded was the right cheek of my derriere. That would have been difficult to explain and somewhat embarrassing.

We had been hitting the enemy on almost a daily basis, pounding them with incendiaries, burning and bombing cities with devastating results. This relentless attack was done in an effort to break the Japanese military who vowed to fight to the last man in defense of their country. Their supply routes had been mined and were all but shut down. Meanwhile, there were shortages of munitions, food and military strength to defend their land. As a result, the Japanese military instructed their people to fight the enemy and defend their country with any means possible. With an invasion of the mainland eminent in the eyes of the Japanese military, they sought to conserve as much munitions as possible for the impeding onslaught. This is, in my opinion, why we faced little to no fighter opposition on many of our bombing raids for the last month or so.

However, on or about the same time, we also began hearing rumors that an invasion of Japan would be necessary, and was almost guaranteed to happen. This was beyond comprehension for most of us as we continued our almost daily raids on the enemy. We knew we were hammering the enemy. Why would we need to invade this country when we were successfully destroying the enemy exclusively through air power? After all, this was the sole purpose of the 20th Air Force and the primary reason for the design and implementation of our aircraft. Was the credo that we had so believed in to this point moot, and what role would we play if this invasion was to take place?

Needless to say, we were not excited regarding the prospects. The entire time we were flying combat missions, we had attained rank commensurate with the number of missions that we flew. This number also had significance for the purpose of your release time. There had been established a rule that after 35 combat missions your obligation to the service would be satisfied and would be sent home. We worried about what was to come and after much talk among ourselves we concluded some logical scenarios of what would take place if there was an invasion. We thought that even those that were close to completion, as I was, would most likely be given a week off and then sent right back in the thick of it to support our ground troops. This was all rumor and speculation on our part, but never the less we were aware of it and wanted to prepare ourselves mentally for it.

Would our credo **"Home Alive in 45, Hell or Heaven in 47"** become a self fulfilling prophecy. We would have to wait and see.

Chapter XXX

Mission:
Raid on Aomori, Japan

July 29th brought yet another incendiary attack, this time on Aomori. This too was an urban city that was clearly devastated by the firebombing tactics that had been so effective in the destruction of Japan. As we dropped 37-500 pound cluster bombs on the city, the place lit up brightly, with more smoke and flames. We were almost without opposition as there was some enemy antiaircraft fire however nothing that came close enough to cause any damage. We continued to blast the enemy and with little opposition our success factor became next to perfect. This was another city that was totally destroyed by fire. This raid took 18 hours to complete.

America knew that Japan was on the verge of defeat and understood that their dedication and culture prohibited them from surrender. They also knew that they had vowed to fight to the last man in defense of their country. This would result in tremendous casualties if we were to invade Japan. The estimates of lives lost in the proposed invasion were in excess of a million men and that cost was too high.

The United States has been working in secret on the Manhattan Project, a nuclear bomb with the capacity of destruction that was unfathomable. Japan had been given the opportunity to surrender but would not accept the terms of an unconditional surrender. They would wait for the inevitable invasion or so they thought.

Chapter XXXI

The Final Missions
Mission:
Raid on Hachioji, Japan

On August 1st and 2nd and we bombed Hachioji another urban area that we just totally destroyed. I think there was a total of close to 200 bombers that participated in this raid, and the target was clearly visible as we dropped our bomb load right on the button. We carried 39-500 pounders that ignited everything in sight. We met no resistance although there was some light flak that we encountered. I didn't see one enemy plane on the entire mission, and our conversation became focused on the end of the war. We got into some discussions on the enemy, and if charges of war crimes would be brought up on the Japanese. The emperor was in control, and what would happen to him. This mission took over 16 hours from start to end, and ended with a fuel stop at Iwo.

The United States had determined it unfortunate but necessary to use its **DOOMSDAY MACHINE** in an effort to finally break the back of the Japanese military. The force of the Atomic bomb would be unleashed on Japan in an effort to spare an invasion and American lives. As a result, this top secret devise had been secretly transported to a location with the capabilities of striking the Empire. It was also determined that the B-29 would be the bomber chosen to deliver this final blow to the Japanese Empire.

August 5th 1945 The Atomic Age

We had gotten back from Iwo and were relaxing for our next raid that was scheduled for August 6th. I was just about to get some shut-eye when the lights on the entire island went off. Everyone was puzzled about what was happening as there were never power outages before. The only time the power would go out was if we were under attack, and that hadn't happened ever on Tinian. The entire island stayed dark for a while, and then I heard a single B-29 firing up, and begin to taxi toward the Northfield runway. We were all puzzled to hear a single B-29 taking, off especially in total darkness, but assumed that some General or supply mission was underway. A few minutes later a few other aircraft took off, and I think I recall a total of three planes took off that evening. Being that we were housed on the other side of the island, I saw the first plane become air-born, but my curiosity ended within a few minutes when the power was back on. It would be years later that we would find out the reason for this.

Mission:
Fire Raid on Saga, Japan

August 6th we raided Saga in another incendiary attack. There were about 60 planes that were involved in this raid and there was considerable flak. We were engaged by an enemy aircraft which had become such a rarity but we lit into him like it was no ones business. We blasted him with machine gun fire and showed the American air superiority. We firebombed the city, fended off the attacking plane, and returned home to Tinian in 16 hours

Earlier in the day, while we were on the mission on Saga, President Truman addressed the nation about the devastation that had been unleashed over Japan. We became aware that the United States had dropped the Atomic Bomb on Hiroshima when we landed, and were debriefed. Never once did we put it together however, the lights out the night before, a lone B-29 on Northfield runway, and the restriction that had been placed on North field. I guess we were too busy fighting the war to take notice. However we were elated to hear that the war might be ending soon.

The next few days were ones of nervous waiting as the United States again offered Japan a means to stopping the war via an unconditional surrender. The devastation of Hiroshima was made evident to us by radio news stations. The entire world knew of a new type of doomsday weapon; the Atomic Bomb, and within days they also knew what the capabilities of its destruction were. There was no mention of the location where it originated, nor was there celebration on our island. It was business as usual when we were awakened early the next morning for a briefing of our next mission

Mission:
Propaganda Leaflet Drop

On August 8th, we flew an early morning mission over Japan. We were all alone, and although we carried no bombs, we were still armed to the teeth with extra ammunition in case we encountered enemy aircraft. Our mission was to drop propaganda leaflets out of our camera hatch, and we let them go for miles and miles.

These leaflets were dropped from late July, until August, and were designed to warn the people of the impending air strikes. They were also meant to encourage evacuation as a means for their personal safety. These leaflets were put out by the United States government and encouraged the Japanese people to read them as the information they possessed could save their lives.

It stated that 4 additionally named cities would be destroyed, as the United States was determined to destroy military installations and all workshop factories producing war tools.

The cities listed contained facilities producing these products, and warned the people to evacuate these cities to save their lives. We did not wish to injure innocent people. It also spoke of America not fighting the Japanese people, but of being engaged in a war with the military clique that had enslaved its people. It also stated that this war, that has so oppressed the Japanese people, will soon be over, and the peace that America will bring would dawn the emergence of a new and better Japan.

The leaflet also addressed the people's role in demanding surrender to their leaders to restore peace, but re-emphasized the impending doom of additional atomic explosions on the cities listed.

What enemy, ever in the history of warfare, had the audacity to name the places that they would attack next. America was so bold that it for warned its enemy, and people of the impending doom, unless they surrender. What a tactic of intimidation, of out and out insolence to the enemy, however they could do nothing to stop us. I am sure that reading such a leaflet infuriated the Japanese military, but to the victor goes the spoils.

In the late afternoon of August 9th, 1945 the city of Nagasaki was hit by yet another atomic explosion, and wiped off the map. We heard confirmation of the assault over the radio, and shared in the exuberance on knowing that the war would soon be over.

Still No Surrender;

Mission:
Target, Hikari Naval Arsenal

On August 14th, with no surrender being called, we continued our assault on the Japanese mainland by raiding the Hikari Naval Yards. We pelted the area, destroying everything in and around the arsenal by blasting them with the 22- 500 pound general purpose bombs we carried. There were many planes on this mission, and surprisingly, we did encounter heavy enemy flak, the likes of which I hadn't seen in a while. Well we slammed the target, and were able to see the intense damage caused by our bombers. We were again unchallenged by enemy fighters, so we took care of business and began the seven hour trip home. The trip home was uneventful, long, tiring and mundane, but as we were within a hundred miles or so of the base, we got the word that everyone had been waiting for.

We were informed of the Unconditional Surrender of Japan!!!

Talk about some broad smiles on our faces, we all were singing and had such happy thoughts of finally being able to go home. We all were so excited that we almost forgot that we were still on a mission, and had to land our plane. We were elated, that we had beaten the odds, brought the enemy to it's knees, and had done it exclusively with air power.

Upon landing, we were still debriefed, and upon completion heard that the emperor of Japan had addressed his people of the surrender via radio. We were told that this was the first time in history the country had ever heard his voice, as he addressed and apologized to the country. He felt responsible for the pain and suffering the Japanese people had endured and would not allow it to continue. This unofficially ended the war on August 15, 1945

114

We had big plans for the future, but at this time, first and foremost was the liberation of our brothers that were still captive in the POW camps. On August 29ᵗʰ we flew to Saipan to pick up relief supplies for our POW's that we would deliver the following morning.

Bright and early we took off on a mission of mercy, to find the hidden POW camps in Japan. We found them alright and began air dropping the much needed medical supplies to our brothers that were now liberated prisoners of war. The POW camp that we delivered to was located on the outskirts of Tokyo and I felt happy in knowing that for the first time, our bomb bays held supplies of food, clothing, and medical supplies for our guys. Cigarettes, water, even candy bars were parachuted into the camps. We flew in at 4,000 feet and as slow as possible as the relief crates began to fall. They dropped on the ground and were immediately pounced upon by waiving GI's. I could see the condition that most were in, and it was evident that these poor guys had been through terrible times. Torn, tattered and malnourished was the overall condition that I witnessed.

That wasn't the half of it as we would later learn of the atrocities they had suffered. They seemed so very uplifted and happy to see us, and were very thankful for the goods. I shared their happiness but also felt the pain and suffering that they were forced to endure. These poor guys knew that the war was over and they had endured, and survived and would soon be home. That mission lasted seventeen hours but that was the best 17 hours I ever spent. We were so glad to bring some comfort and happiness to our fellow GI's.

Years later at a reunion of the 20ᵗʰ Air Force held in Great Bend, Kansas, I had the pleasure of meeting Ray Hap Halloran. Ray has written a book on his endeavors as a P.O.W;

Hap's War. The Incredible Survival Story of a P.O.W. Slated for Execution.

As we spoke of the war, I told him that I had been on a P.O.W. relief mission outside Tokyo on August 30ᵗʰ, 1945 and that coincidently, he had been detained and a prisoner in that very camp. In an emotional reunion, he embraced me, hugging and thanked me for bringing some happiness, cheer, and hope to the freed prisoners. I felt elated, and we both became somewhat emotional reliving those memories. Hap signed my book, and we had a few pictures taken together.

Chapter XXXII

Final Mission:
Tokyo Bay, Fly Over
USS Missouri

Our last mission was over Tokyo Bay on September 2nd, 1945. This would be a historic event and I was going to be a part of it. Some of my buddies and also some other crew members said that it was crazy going on this mission but I had my orders. The main complaint was that we had completed the mandatory combat time, so why push it, and stretch our luck

I thought it to be an honor and privilege to participate in this historical event and so I was part of the group of B-29 Bombers that flew over the USS Missouri during the signing of the peace treaty with Japan. I am proud to be a part of that group of hundreds that flew over head in a show of military strength and numbers during that historic event. Even from the air, it was a spectacular sight to behold and was the official ending of the World War II.

Finally, five days later on September 7th, 1945 we left Tinian on our B-29. This was the day we had all hoped and prayed for. The night before we left, we were all gathered together in the briefing room, as the commanding officer expressed his gratitude and thanks to us all.

He addressed briefly yet sternly on the issue of security. He said,

"If you saw or heard anything, keep your Mouth Shut." Who had the mind set to read into what he was talking about. What did we know, other than the fact that we were getting out of there. It was, **"Home Alive in 45,"** we had made it, we were going home, that was first and foremost on our minds.

I was up bright and early as I had been selected to participate in one of the first waves to be sent home, as I had completed my mandatory 35 missions. I couldn't't wait, to get out of there, and packed my duffle bag full of my cherished belongings as fast as possible, rushing to make the plane. There were 25 men in the plane, with only a few recognizable as crew members, and were all smiles as we became air-born, dreaming of what was to come.

We landed at Kwajalein Island in the Pacific, and as I grabbed my duffle to exit the plane, a wave of panic overcame me. I reached for my Good Luck Hammer, and realized that I hadn't taken it with me. I had left it under my bunk in Tinian. I was saddened but had no recourse to recover it.

The next day, we were onto Hawaii and then to California, USA. From there we boarded a train from California to Andrew's Air Force Base in our nation's capital. During this trip it was the first time that we ever actually got a Pullman Car (sleeping car) for the ride from California to Washington D.C. I guess this was the governments' way of thanking us for a job well done.

On October 25th, 1945 I received my honorable discharge from the US Air Corps and boarded a train for Penn Station Newark, New Jersey. From there I boarded a bus to Paterson and at the station I was greeted by my girlfriend and future wife Theodora (Dot) Stefandelis. I hadn't mentioned it before but we had been writing each other throughout the war. I even had my combat station personalized with **The Jersey Kid and Dot.**

Chapter XXXIII

_____

Back Home in the USA

Having spent more than two years in various locations around the world, almost everything about me had changed. For starters, I had weighed 128 pounds when I was drafted, and had dropped to 113 at the time of my release. Despite my loss of weight, I had grown up quite a bit. I went in an innocent naive 22- year- old and was released at age 24 more worldly but highly nervous. My service to my country had lasted 32 months. Twelve of these months I served overseas seeing, learning, and facing what no man who wasn't there can fully comprehend. But all that was behind me, I had my future to look forward to.

Be it by fate or coincidence, my mandatory 35th missions were completed during the last few days of the war.

The battles and campaigns listed on my Honorable Discharge read: Air Offensive, Japan, China, Eastern Mandates, Central Burma, India and Burma. My decorations and citations read: Asiatic-Pacific Campaign Medal, with one Silver Battle Star, The Good Conduct Medal, The Air Medal with two Bronze Oak Leaf clusters, and the Distinguished Flying Cross. Upon returning to civilian life, I returned back to work as a draftsman at M.W. Kellog Co. in New York City. Facing the challenges of adjustment, as did most veterans, I didn't speak much about what I had been through. This was the time to forget, to heal the raw emotions that we all had suffered.

Not long after I got back to work, early one morning Mr. Shuster, an elderly gentleman and also the chief draftsman, asked me into his office. We sat and talked; all the while I was uncomfortable wondering what this was all about. Having heard of my combat time, he began to question me about my escapades in the war.

I spoke to him of the poverty that I had seen in India and the atrocious living conditions of these poor people. He asked about what it was *really* like over there. I spoke of the people in China, and some incidents that had occurred while I was stationed there. Then, rather abruptly, he interrupted me, looked at his watch, and told me that he had a meeting to go to.

I returned to my drafting table, feeling puzzled about why he had called me there in the first place. It later dawned on me that he wanted to hear stories of combat missions, specifics and all the gory details. Because these were not pleasant memories, I felt it was inappropriate conversation to share with him or for that matter anyone else. How does one explain what it is

118

like to know that any day might be your last, facing an enemy that was barbarous. In risking my life for my country, I had nothing to offer for his amusement.

After having lived first hand through such hardships and through the gut-wrenching hours of some missions, the last thing I wanted to do was to share what I felt during those fearful moments.

I recall once hearing a car backfire, and I jumped, looking for cover. I thought it was an incoming attack. For that second, I was back in the war, bracing for an assault. It was embarrassing because here I was in New York City going out for lunch and I almost dove into the street looking for a fox hole. Luckily, I caught myself and didn't hit the deck

I also think back, overhearing many conversations between people on the commute to and from work right after the war. It was amazing to me that these people were so well versed and authoritative about a war that they had only read about from their newspapers. What was even more galling was the fact that these opinionated people were here in the safety of their home, and were speaking of what tactics that should have been employed. On more than one occasion I was tempted to get up and straighten out these tacticians or as we call them today *Monday Morning Quarterbacks* about the way things really were. What good would that do?!? So I would either move my seat or read the paper because I knew, first hand what it was really like during those fearful missions. I had faced the hell on earth on almost a daily basis and had stuck my neck out, so you could be safe here. I guess living in America entitles each of us the right to voice our opinion, right, wrong, or indifferent.

Some twenty years later, it was released to the general public that the Enola Gay had taken off from Tinian and don't you know it, it was that night that there had been that strange power outage. The black-out that evening twenty years prior was intentional because the scientists were concerned that static electricity might detonate the bomb prematurely. I'm sure security was another factor. Northfield was quite a distance from Westfield where we were housed, but never the less I was right there.

August 9th Bockscar also took off from the same field and dropped the second bomb on Nagasaki, also from North Field, Tinian. It finally dawned on me then that the security the C/O had spoke the night before we were leaving Tinian, was that of the Atomic bomb had been housed and launched from this location. We were told to keep our mouths shut, but were so preoccupied with the thoughts of going home, and being with our families again, that these thoughts never entered our minds.

There was also much information, whether speculative or true, about Emperor Herohito, and the days prior to the surrender. Being the Emperor of Japan, his authority was mostly that of a figure head, and he was not directly involved with the politics or the military in running the country. The Emperor was more like a spiritual leader that legitimatized those that ran the country, and he met with severe opposition on his willingness to surrender. The military did not wish to surrender, and vowed to continue to fight till the last man.

With the second Atomic Explosion over Nagasaki, the Emperor faced the facts that continuing was futile, and was able to convince his adversaries that his people had suffered enough, agreeing to the terms of an unconditional surrender.

I read another article published years after the wars end about the average crew life expec-

119

tancy on missions of B29's bombers flown from Tinian, and the CBI theatre into Japan. This again was years after the war, and I was amazed that the average was only15 missions. Had had I known that then, I would have put in for a transfer, or better yet early retirement.

I married my sweetheart, Dot, right after the war, and became preoccupied with making a living and raising our three children. It wasn't until my retirement that I even thought of those old scrapbooks and in going thru I found my old diary- journal, and I started rethinking about the war. I began to write down some stories.

I began to recall much more about the war and continued to put them to pen and decided to compile them into this book. I still have emotional moments reliving some of those memories. Sometimes a movie, a paragraph of a book or even a certain smell brings me right back in time. I still have the occasional dream about seeing that first Zero coming into my field of vision, my finger hitting the trigger and waking up in a cold sweat.

So at the age of 84, I was determined to complete the project and have a comprehensive review of my experiences in World War II. I wanted to give an accurate account of what it was really like being there. All too often history is written by the tacticians, those that gave the orders and the strategic rational for their decisions. While their accounts of course are extremely important, it is all too often very dry reading. My account is personal, my experiences and perspectives on the many missions I flew, what I saw, felt, and thought. I hope the reader can feel the experience.

To me, this is a catharsis, the hour to finalize all of my experiences, the good, and the not-so good. I have sought to bring to life my visits to distant lands, how it felt all those years ago to see the world for the first time, and to learn and experience new cultures, and new challenges. In overcoming obstacles, fears and sorrows to be among the fortunate to make it home alive.

Although I only have mentioned a few men that gave the ultimate sacrifice for their country, they should never be forgotten, for they are the true heroes.

Looking back, I recall the years prior to my service time and living through the tough times at home. I experienced America, emerging from the Great Depression and times beginning to get better. I also recall that brutal attack on Pearl Harbor and America's declaration of war. I remember the war effort at home, and reading of the German atrocities in Europe. I recall an America, filled with patriotism with flags hung from everywhere and a proud nation coming together under the worst scenario to achieve greatness. I witnessed patriotism, the likes of which I would not see again until after the horrific attack of innocent Americans on September 11, 2001.

In ending I would like to say that I am proud to have served my country, and would do so again, in an instant without hesitation, or resolve.

There are a few memorials for the B29, and I'm proud to be affiliated with them. One is at Great Bend, Kansas, with the names of GI's on it that flew and maintained the Superfortress. Another is at the United States Air Force Academy at Colorado Springs Colorado, and a third is at Bradlee International Airport, Windsor Locks, Connecticut (just outside of Hartford). My name is on all three sites, Sergeant Nick T. Constandelis, 20th Air Force, 58th Bomb Wing, 468th Bomb Group. What beautiful memorials and it is with great honor and privilege that I am associated with such an aircraft. I am proud that my name will be permanently etched in the stone of these memorials as being part of **The Greatest Generation** long after I leave this earth.

May God continue to bless our great country and may we never take for granted our freedom and democracy.

B-29 SUPERFORTRESS MEMORIAL
at the
United States Air Force Academy
Colorado Springs, Colorado

B-29 Air Force Memorial Academy